On Being a Teacher

Books by Jonathan Kozol

Death at an Early Age
Free Schools
The Night Is Dark and I Am Far From Home
Children of the Revolution
Prisoners of Silence

JONATHAN KOZOL

ON BEING
A TEACHER

CONTINUUM • NEW YORK

The Continuum Publishing Company
575 Lexington Avenue, New York, N.Y. 10022

Printed in the United States of America

Kozol, Jonathan.
  On being a teacher.
  Bibliography: p. 167.
  Includes index.
  1. Public schools—United States.
2. Education—United States—Philosophy.
3. Nationalism and education—United States.
I. Title.
LA217.K688   371'.01'0973   80-25950
ISBN 0-8264-0035-3

Acknowledgments

Tisha Graham has worked with me on every page and paragraph of this book. I have relied on her loyalty during endless hours of revision. She has helped me in attempting to make difficult decisions regarding classroom strategies. She has advised me concerning the terrible (but sometimes fascinating) challenges that are encountered every day by conscientious teachers. She has done her best to teach me to write with patience of those with whom I deeply disagree. She is a truthful, totally unselfish woman. I am deeply grateful.

I would also like to thank my fellow teacher Leonard Solo for his loyal support and my patient friends and allies Judith Arnold and Joyce Tatelman, who have typed this book through four revisions. Finally, I thank my mother and my father and my special co-worker Genise Schnitman.

It may be that there is no other way of educating people. Possibly, but I don't believe it. In the meantime it would be a help at least to describe things properly, to call things by their right names. Ideally, what should be said to every child, repeatedly, throughout his or her school life is something like this:

"You are in the process of being indoctrinated. We have not yet evolved a system of education that is not a system of indoctrination. We are sorry, but it is the best we can do. What you are being taught here is an amalgam of current prejudice and the choices of this particular culture. The slightest look at history will show how impermanent these must be. You are being taught by people who have been able to accommodate themselves to a regime of thought laid down by their predecessors. It is a self-perpetuating system. Those of you who are more robust and individual than others, will be encouraged to leave and find ways of educating yourself—educating your own judgment. Those that stay must remember, always and all the time, that they are being moulded and patterned to fit into the narrow and particular needs of this particular society."

The Golden Notebook [1]
Doris Lessing

For this, and all subsequent quotations, references, and items of documentation, see "Notes" in back of book.

Contents

Preface

This is a book for teachers and for those whose children are, for twelve consecutive years, entrusted to their care. In writing all that follows, I have drawn repreatedly upon my own six years in the classroom as a teacher of fourth and fifth grade children and as headmaster of a small and independent urban school, as well as upon a number of other teaching obligations that run the range from pre-college work in Upward Bound to a recent spring semester at South Boston High.

The deepest and most resonant portions of this book, however, depend upon many hundreds of late-night conversations with rank and file teachers. Again and again, at the weary tail-end of a conference, lecture or colloquium, four or five teachers will ask me to sit down and chat. They open up a bottle of wine, or a six-pack of beer, and quietly start to speak about the struggles, fears, dilemmas of a life's career.

Many of these teachers have labored for decades to confront the myths, the tedium and the repetitive humiliations of archaic textbooks and preposterous conventions long-embedded in the written or unwritten rule books of the schools in which they teach. As our late-night meetings continue, I listen to the voices of extraordinary people with a deep tradition of persistence in the face of system-wide timidity and intimidation—teachers who have worked from day to day, and year to year, with neither the glamour of book publication nor the short-lived glow of press or media attention, seldom rewarded in any way at all except perhaps in the one and only way that decent teachers ever find reward: in the gratification of a difficult job done well and in a very basic kind of private dignity courageously upheld.

They work hard, are paid little, but are obliged to contribute almost all their waking hours to the daily task for which they are employed. Virtually any of these teachers could earn more, at less expenditure of time and energy, in almost any other field of intellectual pursuit. Still, they persist.

This book, then, is not only intended for the use of classroom teachers. It is also, and to a very large degree, a compilation of their own views, strategies and ideals. In the long run, it is they—a good deal more than family or TV— who shape the values and establish the competence of the generation now in public school. Their obligation is, for this reason, all the greater—no matter how difficult the task, no matter how high the price or how bewildering the odds.

PART I

Brass Tacks
Strategies for Change

Why Are We Here?
What Is the Job That We
Are Being Asked To Do?

Conscientious teachers who have studied the origins of public education are faced with a difficult and painful choice: If they are honest with themselves and with each other, they cannot help but look upon the public school today as an archaic and dehumanizing institution. This is true not only for the students, but for their teachers also. Students reside within this house of lies for only twelve years at a stretch. Their teachers often are condemned to a life sentence.

Many teachers live and work, as a result, in somewhat the same state of mind as intellectual guerrillas, determined somehow to awaken students, to spark their curiosity and to open up their minds, yet no less determined to *remain* as teachers in the schools. We live and work with a strong resolve to raise some basic, challenging and perhaps subversive questions in the consciousness of children. At the same time we have got to keep in mind the needs of our families, health care, food and mortgage and the rest.

How do we begin? How do we start to free ourselves from impotence and from inertia—in order to be able to fight back?

One logical first step in this process is the effort to desanctify the public school itself as a seemingly immutable sanctuary of some of the most conservative values of the social order. There are dozens of ways to open up this subject in the full view of the class. It can be done by quoting the words of various respected people, such as Horace Mann, who were unhesitant in giving voice to the real purposes of public school. It can be done by giving older students access to a wide array of contemporary books—excerpts, for example, from the words of Edgar Friedenberg, Jules Henry and Paul Goodman, as well as several others who have helped us, as adults, to demystify our own conception of the public schools. It can also be done (and this I believe is the most effective way of all) by sitting down and talking openly with students, in much the way that Doris Lessing recommends.

For those, however, who hesitate to start out with expression of their own opinions, and who prefer to take advantage of provocative quotations from authoritative sources in the present or the past, it is fortunate that some of the most intriguing and revelatory statements happen to derive from unimpeachable, or in any event unquestionably respectable, authorities.

The Board of Education of the state of Arizona, for example, lays it on the line in very brisk, explicit terms. "It is not the job of the schools," the Arizona Board explains, "to create a new social order . . ." The job is "to augment a child's love of country . . . ideals of the home . . . appreciation of traditional values . . ." In another statement, the Arizona Board goes on: "We are proposing a course of study for American children . . ." The document explains our obligation to enable children to appreciate "the nature of national power . . ." The consequence of this education, we are told, ought to be a recognition of those forces which could undermine our nation, in order that students "may recognize and . . . thwart such threats . . ." The final result which Arizona teachers are expected to achieve includes, above all else, a recognition that our nation is "the envy of the civilized world . . . the last best hope of mankind . . ."[2]

There is no pretense here of going to school to learn to be a sensitive, loving or compassionate person, nor one who is concerned in any way at all about those people who do not live in this nation but who, nonetheless, in the opinion of most teachers and their students, still may seem to hold some claims upon our loyalty as human beings.

However we do it, I believe it is our job to make quite clear to students that schools exist precisely in order to destroy such loyalty: to lead us to conceive an evil "differential" in the worth of human life, depending on whether that life is white, American, Nordic, Western European, or whether—in contrast—it is the life of someone black or brown, Third World or socialist, or, in any event, "not like our own."

Teachers who do no more than find and make available to pupils a number of forceful quotations on this subject, but do not choose to underline the fact that tragic actions (My Lai, for example) are the direct result of education of this kind, have got to face the fact that most of their students will protectively absorb these statements back into the undisturbing matrix of a lifetime of parental bias, TV pacification and eleven other years of public school indoctrination which either precede or follow those few months in which our pupils have a chance to look into our eyes and (sometimes) hear our views. We have no choice, therefore, if we should wish to make our point both unforgettable and clear, but to add something of our own conviction to the words we quote from others.

I spoke above of Massachusetts educator Horace Mann. Mann's views are in painful accord with those of the Arizona Board of Education, although his most disarming words speak less about political indoctrination than about another major function in our public schools: class stratification. In a report to the Massachusetts Board of Education in 1844, he made it all too clear: "Finally, in regard to those who possess the largest shares . . . of wordly goods, could there, in your opinion, be any police so vigilant and effective, for protection of all the rights of person, property and character, as such a . . .

system of common schools could be made to impart. . . . Would not the payment of a sufficient tax to make such education and training universal, be the cheapest means of self-protection and insurance?"[3]

Here again, I see no reason why a teacher ought to hesitate to make quite sure that the children wholly understand what Horace Mann has said. His name is carved in granite on the front of schools all over the United States. His words (*protection* and *insurance*), therefore, are very much like precious gems to those who wish to clarify this point. Students who are only in the sixth or seventh grade, however, are likely to lose themselves in his elaborate syntax. I don't believe that any sensible person is going to accuse a teacher of manipulative imposition if all we do is to make sure that children really get the point of these extraordinary words.

Another man whom teachers might do well to quote (and whom, of course, they would be able to quote with absolute impunity from potential adversaries) is the twenty-eighth president of our nation, Woodrow Wilson. "We want one class of people to have a liberal education, and we want one class of persons, a very much larger class of persons, of necessity, to forego the privileges of a liberal education and fit into specific manual tasks."[4] How can a school board which professes to respect American tradition plausibly seek to reprimand a teacher who relies upon the words of Woodrow Wilson?

The reason for quoting educators such as Horace Mann— still better, a distinguished president of the United States—is in order to protect ourselves against malicious and destructive criticism. A lot of other people, such as Upton Sinclair and Jack London, say very much the same things Woodrow Wilson did. But why go out and hunt up radical and angry writers when the men who run this nation state it all so well themselves? Those who fight a battle of whatever kind against a powerful foe often find that one of the most effective strategies is to steal into the weapons warehouse of those who hold the reins of power and obtain their ammunition there. The words of people such as Woodrow Wilson represent precisely the kind of ammunition that I have in mind.

If school, as Horace Mann insists, is meant to be "the cheapest means" of self-protection for the rich, then students ought to know this early in the game—while they are still in school—not once it is all over. John Kenneth Galbraith has observed that mass deception seldom works so well once people understand that it is taking place.

Another way to underline this point about the actual as opposed to the mythical objectives of our public schools is to draw the parallel to a "consumer fraud." Schools are the fourth biggest business in the nation. (Defense, "the readiness for war," comes first.) Like many other business enterprises in this nation—food producers, for example, and the supermarket chains—schools are guilty of most of the major facets of consumer fraud: false labels, dangerous content and half-empty boxes.

Schools advertise a lot of sweet and optimistic things: truth and beauty, the pursuit of greater insight into our own soul, "a search for humane values in a troubled time"—along with a couple of good old-fashioned things like basic skills. That, at least, is what the label says. Inside the box, too often, what we find is just exactly what the founders of our public education system said that we would find: class stratification and political indoctrination. For many teachers, the example of consumer fraud provides a very simple means by which to make a complicated point more clear: School advertises one thing, sells another. In any other realm of life, this would be castigated and forbidden.

Issues like these can be conveyed to students without the use of radical rhetoric—and also without the attribution of "conspiracy" to any sinister or demonic force. Rich men and women, school board members, textbook editors—and the people at the State Department and the C.I.A.—don't need to meet each other in a secret bunker beneath the mountains of Montana every year in order to decide the way to fry the brains of little kids and stamp a patriotic imprint in between their eyes. The reason they don't need to meet or to conspire is quite clear: They share most of the same self-serving values as the consequence of their own long period of years in public school. Those who have so much in common to defend by law-mandated lies do not need to meet in secret hiding places in Montana.

To make this point in front of students—and to try at the same time to steer away from ominous talk of "ruling-class oppression" and the like—seems to me a useful way to ward off criticism from those who otherwise may try to slot us, in a simpleminded way, as "troublemakers." In honest fact, we *might* be, but we are certainly not simpleminded or dogmatic. And we are a great deal more effective, I believe, as a direct result.

Whenever I have the chance to speak with pupils in the public schools, I do my best to emphasize a fact that schools do everything they can to lead us to forget: Public schools did not exist forever. They did not come out of the forehead of a Greek or Roman god. They were contrived by men and women—ordinary, sometimes clever, sometimes not so clever, men and women—and, for just this reason, they can be rebuilt or reconceived, dismantled or replaced, not by another set of gods, but by plain men and women too.

A teacher might speak to students in such simple words as these: "Anything that was first contrived by men and women can be taken apart or thrown away by men and women also. It isn't unchangeable. It isn't inexorable. You and I can leave school as it is, can change it slightly, or else we can turn it inside out and upside down."

If a teacher does say something of this sort to students, certain people will probably protest that children should not be compelled to hear this kind of talk when they are still so young. I disagree: Why should we wait until our students are as weary, weak and soul-broken as we, before we dare to tell them what it's all about?

It may be that school manipulation will no longer work once students have a chance to see it for exactly what it is. Those who tell us we should wait "another year or more" before we speak of matters of this kind are usually those who wish that we would wait forever.

Why should we delay in areas so basic to the truth we wish to live by—or the lies that presently degrade us and our pupils too?

2

First Person Singular—and Plural

In order to be able to achieve the sense of inner leverage to perceive the schools as institutions we have power to transform, students and teachers need to feel they have the right, the license and the sanction to speak out in the first person plural: "we." People, however, cannot easily say "we" if they do not first achieve the sense of self-possession to say "I."

Schools, by tradition, do all that they can to train us *not* to speak in the first person. In the classic situation in the elementary grades, if a child speaks in rude, impatient words to a school teacher, there is a stock response that comes out often in a kind of singsong. "Is that any way," the teacher asks, "to speak to me?" Instead of saying *me,* however, teachers often seem to step away and speak as if they had replaced themselves by someone else: "Is that any way to speak to . . . Miss O'Brien?"

It is, for just one moment, as if she were not "in presence" in the room, but locked up somehow in the closet with the chalk and chalk-erasers. In the universities and high schools, we hear the same thing—for example, in those "regulations for term papers" which instruct the students to avoid the sound of their own voice: "The paper should have a clearly indicated introduction, body and conclusion. Do not use the word *I* except in the conclusion . . ."

It is as if the students can't admit that they are *there* until they are about to leave the room. It is the ideal language for an alienated people in a mechanistic land. Those who do not know that they exist, and live, and breathe, in the first person are the perfect workers to press buttons on sophisticated instruments in vast and modern industries of war—or else to press those buttons that release the bombs and napalm on defenseless villages in foreign nations.

Pilots and presidents who live and breathe in the third person can make the gruesome choice to wipe out a whole continent, destroy a population or obliterate a city with a single weapon, then go to bed and sleep for eight good hours in uninterrupted peace. It isn't just a foolish English lesson, then. It is something far more frightening and more disturbing.

One of the ways by which a teacher can begin to fight this myth, right in the context of the public school, is by providing students with direct, exciting access to the words, the voices, the whole manner of self-presentation, of some of those men and women in our own or former times who have been able to transcend this inhibition and who do, as a direct result, feel power to speak out in their own words and to regain the sense of their own voice.

"In most books, the 'I', or first person, is omitted. In this [book,] it will be retained." These words are from the first page of *Walden* by Thoreau. That, he says, is "the main difference" between his own book and those of other writers.

There will be dozens of other examples of this willingness to speak out in first person pronouns in the later sections of this book. Merely to quote from famous people is, however, less effective, in my own belief, than another method which many teachers put into effect without a tactical intent, but pretty much by nature. This is—in a literal sense—to learn to speak out and to *be,* an open and at all times undisguised "first person," exemplified in the very ways that we behave with students and in the words we choose to speak in the course of conversations with them.

I do not mean simply that we ought to be prepared to state our own opinions within earshot of our pupils (although I do mean this, as well), but that we also need to be first persons in the eyes of children in the deeper sense of letting all our own complexities, our viewpoints, hesitations, dreams and passions—and our vulnerable aspects, too—become apparent to the class.

I think that many seasoned teachers will perceive in this a recommendation which is far more subversive than it may at first appear. It is subversive both of the age-old school tradition of professional behavior on the part of educators and also—sad to say—of many teachers' age-old concept of *themselves*. Few of us are encouraged, in the course of teacher preparation, to grant ourselves the luxury of being just plain human beings within the eyes of children.

The concept of professional behavior, as it has been defined for fifty years in public education, is devoid of almost all intensities. The teacher does not easily yield to indignation, weep for passion, rage at grief. All that we love in drama, all that we find breathtaking in a film, all that is tragic, comic, intense, extreme, remarkable, is filtered from the teacher's manner. If film and drama were restricted to the range of feelings present in this type of classroom, the theaters would quickly empty and the people would pour out on the streets. Only the schools command a captive box office, because attendance at their presentation is compulsory.

Sometimes, seeing the traditional grade-school teacher standing there within that room, blackboard behind her, chalk dust about her, one wonders what would happen if, for a terrible moment, she should lose control, forget herself—and swear. Swear right there, in front of the class, like ordinary people do, without the time to qualify her words. Would the children smile? Would she be smiling too? It seems at times as if the sky will break in pieces, the roof collapse and the walls come down in timbers if the teacher, walking across the room before the class, should bang her knee on the edge of a table and it should start to bleed. One wonders if, perhaps, it wouldn't even bleed—not like the knees of other people. If it did bleed, it would tell the children she was human.

The professional inhibition I have just described is one that was carefully molded and foisted upon us by successive generations. It is a pattern which self-respecting teachers will no longer tolerate today, and everyone who cares for kids *and* teachers—as well as for the future of American education— must rejoice as a result.

In making this statement, I do not intend to recommend, instead, the whimsical and irresponsible behavior which was identified with the counterculture of ten years ago. This sort of behavior (exemplified often in a slipshod manner and a disrespectful style of dress) seems to me, indeed, almost more dangerous than the style it was intended to replace. Moreover, it cannot conceivably win us allies where we need them most. It either alienates or, at least, disquiets many parents who might otherwise have given us support.

I do believe, however, that we ought not to be scared to let our real emotions show—to do so, moreover, every bit as openly with our students as we would with our adult friends, our families and (if we have children) our own kids.

There are certain instances, of course, when teachers have excellent reason to conceal particular aspects of their lives, not only from their pupils but from anyone at all; there is no reason on earth why teachers ought to feel compelled to share *all* of their private feelings with their pupils in ways they would not do even with adult friends. But teachers also have the right to laugh, the need to cry, to demonstrate anger, pain, anxiety or fear, right in the classroom just as openly as they might do in their own homes. We do not make ourselves professionals by rendering all our motions stiff and wooden—and our humor or exhilaration rigid and unreal. Teachers can weep when we are mourning someone we have loved, and we can tell our children we are feeling rotten if we just wake up one morning and feel sick. There is no reason why we have to tell the class we need to "wash our hands" or "freshen up" if what we really need to do is use the toilet; nor is there a reason why we cannot swear like hell if, by bad luck, we should fall down and twist our leg or bang our knee.

Teachers can bleed in every way, inside and out, and students should know it; they will not hate us as a consequence, because they bleed as well. They suffer too, and do not simply need to "freshen up" when they request permission to "go down the hall." They sweat also, often laugh, and sometimes need to weep.

This is, I think, the most important way of all by which we teach our pupils the power and license to speak out, and cry, and breathe, and live, and love—and someday struggle—in first person pronouns: first to say "I" and one day to say "we."

3

Extreme Ideas

Often, if a student tries to give expression to a strong belief, especially if that student states his views in terms that seem to lead in the direction of a real dispute, teachers tend, by an automatic reflex, to try to cool things off and to persuade the student to tone down his views: "Peter, isn't that a bit strong?"

If the student agrees to backtrack and retreat, then he often wins respect or even praise for self-control: "That sounds more sensible."

In actual fact, and by direct result, as there comes to be *less to believe,* the teacher says it sounds increasingly believable. The same thing happens with a strong opinion which has not been rounded off to fit the class consensus: "Okay . . . David says that black Americans are now fighting for their rights . . . and Susan says that we need law and order. . . . Well . . . there might be truth in *both* of these positions . . ." Long pause. At last the resolution: "Why don't we see if we can't find a *third* position?"

The teacher seldom comes right out and states the truth: "Look, we're going to have an easier time together if you'll just cut back on your convictions for a little while." Instead, there is the absolute suggestion that the third position is *more true* than either of the two extremes: that truth lives "closer to the middle."

One consequence of this idea is the viewpoint, reinforced by many modern school materials, even of the most sophisticated kind, that anger, conflict, confrontation of all kinds are nothing more than a perceptual mistake: "Nobody really disagrees with someone else once we have explained ourselves with proper care." Hence, the new and profitable field of bogus classroom ethics known as "conflict resolution" or as "clarification" of our values and our former points of view. The message of this new material is clear: Confrontation is perceived as if it were the consequence, in almost every case, of poorly chosen words or of inadequate perception: "We have to learn not just to talk, but also how to listen, how to understand . . ." The message here is that, if we learn to listen well, we will not hear things that we do not like. To hear things that we do not like is to hear incorrectly.

There are these words in the Bible: "Where there is no vision, the people perish." A vision is, by definition, both expansive and extreme. It is, precisely, the exclusion of the vision from the public classroom—and, in particular, from the inner-city school—which guarantees that apathetic mood, those arid and unstimulating class discussions, so easily mistaken by observers for "a lack of pupil motivation."

It is not simply a case of pedagogic styles that fail to elicit the intensities and emotions of our pupils. It is, rather, a case of school-mandated *absence of intensity* which has successfully *excluded* such emotion. The conventional wisdom of the U.S. public school is the virtue of the low-key, the cautious, the consensus view. Because a vision of justice is incompatible with such a preference, the students have learned, long years before the secondary grades, to leave their sense of passion at the classroom door.

The bias against extremes is paralyzing in its impact on the teacher and the student both. All intense ideas or radical views are treated as inherently suspect, while moderate statements ("notions," not "convictions") are given credence from the start. The term *radical* is universally described in textbooks as a sickly aberration of a healthy state of mind called *liberal*. In the same sense, *revolution* is defined as an unwholesome word, an agonized distortion of a healthy term: *reform*.

There is a phrase, consistent with this view, found often in the textbooks, press and magazines: "extremists on both sides." The purpose of this phrase is to make people believe that there is something evil, in all cases, in extreme ideas. This, clearly, is not so. Extreme devotion, for example, to the implementation of the details of annihilation of the Jews is not the same as an extreme determination to assassinate the Nazi leaders. "Extremists on both sides" is a deceptive phrase. It tries, once more, to get a student to believe that there is always more truth sitting someplace in the middle. It also tries to get a child to believe that there must *be* a genuine "middle" every time. This, too, is simply not the case.

A ruling principle, in many high school texts, goes somewhat in these terms: "All extremes of action or belief are equally unwise. Sooner or later, all will lead to self-betrayal, self-corruption or deceit."

The Soviet Union is the traditional example of the failure or inevitable distortion of extreme beliefs. The textbooks never speak of the extreme success of that most memorable revolution that took place two hundred years ago in the United States, nor of the extreme importance of the revolution which is, in a sense, still taking place today in Shanghai and Peking. Nor do they speak of the extreme ideas of Malcolm X, Saint Francis or Saint Joan.

The truth is that extreme reaction to extreme ordeal is not only healthy and intelligent at times, but also very often the sole ethical response of honorable people in the face of human pain. How can we begin to render this unpopular point of view both potent and persuasive to our students?

My own approach is to confront the issue head-on, in subjective terms, by stating some of these arguments to children outright, much as I have stated them right here, and as we all do with one another in the real world. Many teachers, however, will probably react to this suggestion much as they have done before. They will ask why we must *state* such matters to the class when, instead, with richly assorted data scattered all around the room, the children can discover all of this themselves? Although this is a method that I always find peculiarly circuitous, I see no reason to object to teachers who prefer this means of getting an idea across to children. I simply think that we are being far more candid if, at least at some point in the game, we state it in our own words, too.

The other approach, delineated above, is to make available a broad array of relevant quotations of a number of "extreme" ideas and points of view, stated by people like Tom Paine and Thomas Jefferson, for instance—people whom the textbooks have already taught the children to revere.

"The tree of liberty must be refreshed from time to time with the blood of patriots and tyrants."[5] Jefferson wrote these words in 1787. Many teachers nowadays discover that direct quotations of that kind—drawing on the real (extreme) beliefs of highly reputable and patriotic people—tend to stir up an extreme response in children, while simultaneously they leave the teacher partially protected from attack.

William Lloyd Garrison, the abolitionist who lived and wrote in Boston over a century ago, also spoke about the matter of extreme reactions in dramatic terms. Asked by a friend why he was "all on fire" with his rage, Garrison replied: "I have need to be all on fire, for I have mountains of ice about me to melt."[6]

Henry David Thoreau, whose quotations and convictions recur (and will recur) again and again within this book, is a man I take to be a model of straightforward talk and of unhesitant denunciation of whatever it was that passed for conventional wisdom in his time. He proved also to be indignant and remarkably unbridled in defense of a style of speech for which he would be graded very, very low in all too many of the U.S. public schools.

"I fear chiefly," Thoreau stated in 1854, "lest my expression may not be *extra-vagant* enough. . . . I desire to speak somewhere *without* bounds." [7]

Of all such expressions of conviction on this subject, the one I like the most is that of Martin Luther King. In "Letter from Birmingham Jail" (1963), [8] he wrote these words: "Was not Jesus an extremist for love? . . . The question is not whether we will be an extremist, but what kind of extremist we will be. Will we be extremists for hate or will we be extremists for love? Will we be extremists for the preservation of injustice or will we be extremists for the cause of justice?"

Apart from straight quotation, there are also many concrete and well-documented cases of extreme behavior, based upon extreme belief, which did not lead into a self-destructive or corrupting end result. What if, for instance, teachers were prepared to put aside the obvious betrayal of the dream within the U.S.S.R. and to speak instead of the extreme success of public education in post-revolutionary Cuba or of the extreme success of health care in post-revolutionary China? In order to do this, teachers need to have good—indeed, impeccable—data and resources. The rebel, here as in almost all other situations, must be an infinitely more careful scholar than the writer or speaker of innocuous and inoffensive views. I have tried to give a lot of leads for interesting and helpful source materials in the final pages of this book.

The ultimate approach in attacking this dilemma is not the lesson of "the right quotation," nor of "the right example" from the distant past. It is the power of the teacher to articulate a point of view in words of passion equal to the substance which those views convey. This alone provides a class of students with an inviolable precedent for honest exposition of their own intense beliefs. A teacher who reverts, in every case, to colorless understatement and to oblique expressions of belief cannot offer pupils any credible lessons in the virtues of outspoken, lucid or extreme ideas.

The hidden curriculum, as we have seen before, is the teacher's own integrity and lived conviction. The most memorable lesson is not what is written by the student on a sheet of yellow lined paper in the lesson pad; nor is it the clumsy sentence published (and "illustrated") in the standard and official text. It is the message which is written in a teacher's eyes throughout the course of his or her career.

It is the lesson which endures a lifetime.

4

Disobedience Instruction

One of the most effective inhibitions planted in the conscious-ness of students and teachers in our public schools is a sel-dom-stated yet remorseless sense of terror at the possibility of *saying no*.

Textbooks achieve this goal by use of various time-honored and, by now, almost unnoticed methods of dogmatic certitude and condescension. They do it also by the use of small catch-phrases which are contrived to frighten students into blind ac-ceptance of an adult point of view. When, at times, a student does break out in clear-cut condemnation of a text or an idea, there is a stock response. Students are accused of being "neg-ative"—or of "making unconstructive comments."

There is some paradox in this. Americans would not be the citizens of a land called the United States at all if a number of rebels such as Sam Adams, Thomas Jefferson, Tom Paine and several thousand more had not been extremely "negative" in their viewpoints on King George III—and offered to suggest *no* "positive" alternatives.

Students in the early grades of school, if they are bright enough to recognize the devious materials that fill their texts and readers, and blunt enough to speak of it out loud, often are contained or silenced by another familiar manner of suppression: "Let's not be negative or hostile. Let's not indulge in unconstructive criticism. Why don't we try to find the good points in the story?" This litany of seductive affirmation leads, too often, to another pattern of familiar words: "It isn't right to knock things down unless we are prepared to put up *new* things in their place."

There are innumerable variations on these words: "A great many people worked for a long, long time to write these stories for us, and to draw these illustrations, and to print this book. . . . It's all very easy for a little boy or little girl to criticize the work of someone else without suggesting something better."

This is, of course, an unjust argument. All of us have the right to criticize what we detest, whether or not we have the skill to "make a better one" ourselves. Patients in the hospital have an unquestioned right to voice their protest if a surgeon seems about to make use of a rusty scalpel, even if those patients cannot claim to do the surgery themselves. In the same sense, students who do not know the way to write, to print, to illustrate and bind a polished substitute for the fourth-grade reader, should not let an adult take away their right to speak with anger of a book they feel to be dishonest—or just dull.

There is an unspoken agenda in these curious clichés: Whenever students are told they do not have the right to knock down an idea (or to attack a book) unless they are prepared to offer up an instantaneous replacement, there is the message, tucked between the lines, that there has got to *be* a "something better" every time. It is as if a builder were to put up a gigantic A & P right in the middle of a beautiful green valley in the state of Maine, then were to look his critics in the eyes and ask us if we think that we can build a better one ourselves.

Words like these lead people to forget that there was once a time when they could stand and look across unspoiled land and see the blue-green line of the horizon. Everything does not need an alternative suggestion. Some things need not to exist at all.

Many teachers, in frustration, have resorted to a number of ingenious methods to subvert this myth. Some teachers do it by the presentation of a simple line of logic: describing, for example, the imagined situation of the patient underneath a rusty scalpel, or of a small village of poor people in the face of a huge and irresponsible construction firm.

Other teachers have made extensive use of major news reports—those, for example, which were generated by the events at Watergate or Three Mile Island. Both are situations where the inability of well-trained American adults to *say no* to an ongoing process of deceit, or of progressive self-deceit, has led to tragic consequences, not just for those who were the victims, but also (in one way or another) for themselves. Events in the more distant past (the bombing of Hiroshima, for example) provide a teacher with even stronger historical evidence to reinforce the point. Again, as before, there is no need to search for radical sources of reproach if the strongest evidence is already present in the daily press.

A teacher might line up, in opposite columns on a ditto sheet, certain statements published in their textbooks praising the virtues of acquiescence, of obedience and of "positive ideas" and, on the other side, the courtroom testimony of those ordinary but pathetic figures who went into Watergate to steal, into My Lai to kill—among other reasons, because they lacked the power to *say no.*

There is a verse which, up until recent years, was contained within the official curriculum of the Boston Public Schools: "Every day, in every way, / it is our duty to obey."[9] A teacher might take this rhyme and line it up, along with a number of comparable quotations, on the left side of a page. On the right side, we might display some of the words of American soldiers who (as we might carefully remind each student) were the products of a school "just like our own."

Many teachers—without suggestion from me or any other writer—have, for several years already, made highly effective and always upsetting use of quoted words from Adolf Eichmann, whose own preparation for obedient behavior was received in German public schools. Teachers might point out, as well, that our own schools were modeled on the German system more than a century ago and that both systems have quite similar objectives: the education of "good Germans," or "good citizens," as we in the United States would say.

"I was only obeying my orders," Eichmann said. What other lesson could he possibly have learned within a well-run public school?

Again, I believe it is our special obligation to make certain that the point at stake cannot conceivably be blurred. "Normal" American students, after all, already sufficiently socialized by their prior years in public school, have a powerful vested interest in attempting to avoid the real significance of our references to Eichmann or to Hiroshima.

"Do you get the point?"

I have often asked this question in the presence of a high school class. I do not pretend that there is *not* "a point." I do not pretend that I have no idea of what conclusion my pupils might possibly "discover." Nor do I pretend that every possible conclusion might be "equally correct." I do not turn the class into a preplanned guessing game ("discovery method") by which to direct students to my own conclusion. I do not renounce my adult judgment and pretend I have no serious objectives of my own.

"There *is* a point. Dumb, dangerous rhymes like those our school supplies to us have led a lot of people just like you into some tragic acts of theft or murder. Blueprints, alternatives and optional suggestions are all fine and good; but there are also moments when a well-planned act of straight refusal and denunciation proves to be a lot more useful and important to the preservation of the human race. I would like it very much if I could leave you, by the year's end, with the courage to say no, in spite of all the doubts and inhibitions which will always be within you."

There are, however, as we have seen, certain teachers who prefer to quote from others rather than to say these things themselves. Instead of speaking out in their own voice, such teachers prefer to make certain that the writings of many different kinds of moral and political rebels are available and constantly accessible to students. Moreover, they make certain that the relevant writings are displayed in such a way as to advertise themselves. The writings of distinguished social critics are spread out across the tables and display racks of the classroom, not crowded onto shelves or packed in cartons.

My own belief, repeated often in this book, is that a teacher's stated views—and, more important, the visible actions which that teacher takes during a year in public school—are infinitely more relentless in their impact on the students than a wealth of books of any possible variety. More powerful still is the degree to which a class of children comes to feel that it is safe to say no even to the teacher. Since students have learned for years that this, of all denunciations, is the one most to avoid and fear, it is also the one which is most difficult to batter down.

In trying to make this mode of thought and of denunciation even conceivable among the students I have taught, I have sometimes opened the semester by announcing to the class that we would be involved, for several days, in something that I call "Disobedience Instruction."

Grade-school children at times appear alarmed by the idea. It takes a bit of work to make it clear that I do not intend to urge them to go home and be malicious to their folks, nor do I hope that they will feel the urge to be malicious here in school. I draw a line, as well as I can, between two very different states of mind: the sheer vindictive malice of defiance and aggression on the one hand, and a vigorous note of ethical irreverence on the other. The first attacks the person, while the second concentrates on that person's viewpoints and beliefs.

There is another reason why the line has to be drawn between our criticism of another person's views and an attack upon that person's heart and soul. In order for a student to be able to believe that it is safe to say no to a teacher, it is important that the student feels that he or she will not be subject to retaliation. If there is not a clear distinction made between a person's words and his or her own inner self, then students often seem to feel that they cannot attack the words a teacher speaks without, in essence, striking at the teacher too.

Even worse, students will find it difficult to believe that teachers can do combat with a student's views without thereby reflecting a deep-seated anger at the student also.

To begin the class with a discussion about honest disagreement seems to me to be the logical way for us to start. It enables students to engage in sharp disputes that bring their thought and feeling to a strong insistent pitch, yet also enables them to feel entire safety at the hands of teachers—or the class itself.

Schools tend to steer away from heated disputations of the kind I have in mind, fearing (as one handbook[10] of the N.E.A. has put it) that emotion-charged issues "may lead to an argument so explosive that fighting can result." (We are so far from this eventuality today that teachers—plagued for ages with the undevoted apathy of mediocre class discussion— might very well get up and cheer if anyone in their class should ever care enough to throw a spitball in defense of an idea!) Students, in my experience, are wholly capable of learning to say no, with both control and dignity, not only to each other but to adults too, and to the teacher first of all, and to distinguish between anger at a person's point of view and hatred for the person who expressed it.

This, to me, seems an essential precondition in a classroom where the teacher plans to take a controversial stand on serious ideas. If the students can't say no (or think somehow that they'd better not for their own personal well-being), then the teachers find themselves in a restrictive situation. Their power, being irrefutable, is limitless. Their viewpoints, being past all disputation, come to be totalitarian.

Again—apart from all the words that we can speak in this regard, and even apart from all the various people we can quote to give our students precedent for courage and denunciation in the face of our own views—the very best lesson of all is *demonstration.* Teachers can demonstrate the point in obvious ways: by their own disobedience of a supervisor or a school board, for example. This, however, is an action that many teachers may well judge to be unwise for obvious reasons of survival, at least in the early years of their career. Another method, therefore, far less dangerous and more direct, is to invite another teacher into class, someone who disagrees with you on a dead-earnest issue, then do your best to start a heated disagreement with that teacher.

Students who have been taught to think, "The teacher's always right," are faced with a dilemma when two teachers disagree. The students know both people can't be right, yet both are teachers and both are adults. The lesson seems to set at least two useful precedents.

First, it shatters the idea that teachers can't be wrong, giving the students more reason to dissent with *either* teacher in the months and years ahead.

Second, it demonstrates that people can dissent with great intensity and still retain respect for one another.

The open disputation of two teachers, in the full view of the class, no matter how unconventional or unexpected, proves repeatedly to be a lively catalyst for students who are otherwise reluctant to come out with their own views. Once the students see their teachers in articulate dispute, the idea of infallibility is gone for good. From that point on, students are able to speak with full irreverence, but without the terror of retaliation. Teachers, as a result, are freed at last from arid imitations of neutrality.

Needless to say, this kind of work is seldom part of the traditional curriculum within the public schools. In the wake of the decade of Watergate, however—not even to speak of recent revelations of government-authorized and possibly organized duplicity, actions of cover-up and collusion in Miami by the courts and the police, the multiple and apparently unabated plottings of the C.I.A. (plottings which too many people now unhappily accept as part of our national self-interest) or the slow, unceasing radioactive leakage of contaminated wastes throughout our land, followed by the grotesque denial of such dangers by the very corporations that are most involved—it may well be that the courage of unabated indignation and denunciation is the most important single lesson that remains within our power to convey to children in the public schools.

It would be overly optimistic to predict that hundreds of thousands of teachers, in the next few years, are likely to adopt these strategies without grave hesitation. It is the truth, however, that hundreds of teachers in the past few years have already begun to seize upon this frank approach as the one most elemental lesson they can offer to their pupils in the first weeks of the year.

It calls for just as much work, in a nation like our own, to return to kids the license to *say no* as it required once, in an earlier age, to take that privilege away.

5

Women in History, but not in Public School: Some Ways of Fighting Back

For generations women have been treated with contempt, or else relegated wholly to oblivion, within the U.S. public schools.

In most textbooks it appears that great, heroic or courageous women don't exist at all. Those few who do are almost always dull and unexciting people, seldom important on their own, but famous only for their luck in being married to a famous man. Martha Washington and Mary Todd Lincoln are two obvious examples. The black leader Harriet Tubman receives a little better treatment than the rest, but even she tends to be drained or sanitized of nine-tenths of her most serious beliefs.

The one woman who appears in every textbook under her own steam is the patriotic seamstress, Betsy Ross. This choice, on the part of textbook authors, no longer comes to many teachers as a great surprise. Nothing could be more perfect, and predictable, than that the school boards should select as token woman of the U.S. public schools a person whose only competence falls squarely in that area of women's work known as "homemaking skills." Others of that era who were independently significant (Abigail Adams, for example) either are ignored completely or else given token mention at the most.

Even now, two centuries since the U.S. revolution, none of this has greatly changed. Most of the exciting women of the past one hundred years—Dorothy Day, Susan B. Anthony and Emma Goldman are just three examples—seldom are even named in public school. Teachers (above all, women teachers who have had to live with this bias for a lifetime) know very well the reason why the women I have named are bypassed totally in public school. Each of them represents a vigorous example of unfrightened women—liberated not just (as women) from manipulation by male leaders, but also (as passionate and indignant human beings) from the domination of a nation's lies and from the power of the major corporations.

Susan B. Anthony and Emma Goldman have been dead for many years—Dorothy Day only since the winter of 1980. Her death (on December 1st) came in her eightieth year. She was a devoutly religious woman who believed that the best way to be Christian is to practice Christ's ideals by standing up for those who are most poor and hungry.

In order to demonstrate her faith by visible witness, Dorothy Day participated in countless protest actions, fasted for weeks and even months, and went to prison many times. She also traveled to Cuba to learn first-hand about the Cuban revolution. When the migrant workers in the fields of California went on strike in 1973, merely for recognition of their right to have a union, Dorothy Day went out to join them on the picket lines, despite the fact that she was then well over seventy. When the police began to make arrests, she refused to step aside. She was arrested and later imprisoned with the workers.

For nearly fifty years, Dorothy Day, with the help of many friends of various religious views and political persuasions, edited and published a monthly paper called *The Catholic Worker*. The paper costs a penny a copy, as it did right from the start. It is a unique newspaper—independent in its views, full of a fascinating mix of political stories, personal diaries and reflections on (and sometimes by) the multitude of homeless people who were attracted to the house in which its editor lived and died.

Because the paper is never restricted by a single line or dogma, it does not automatically oppose all socialist ideas the way most other U.S. papers do. As a result, *The Catholic Worker* comes out with a number of well-documented stories that are seldom covered in the ordinary press: whether it is a story about a staff member's travels to a previously forbidden nation like Vietnam or else a purely impressionistic story of the life and death of men and women in the Lower East Side neighborhood of New York City where the staff of the paper has resolved to make its home.

Dorothy Day is viewed by many people as a saintly rebel. She never hesitated to speak in favorable terms of many revolutionary struggles in the Third World, even though she was a pacifist herself. Women with her unusual persistence are regarded as subversive people by the U.S. schools. Textbooks have managed to guarantee that students do not hear about a woman like Dorothy Day. Now that she is dead, and after fifty years go by, then perhaps she will receive her place in the curriculum—but, most likely, not for her authentic views. She will become another plastic heroine: empty of content, and scrubbed clean of real belief.

A standard question comes to mind as soon as we try to speak of people such as Dorothy Day: How can teachers possibly cope with areas of gross evasion that are both so sweeping and so vast—especially if they have no other materials at hand than what the school board gives them? It is for this reason that I have supplied a number of suggestions for additional reading in the end matter of this book. Many teachers also emphasize that the major lessons in regard to women ought to start, not with a list of famous people, but right in their own classroom in discussion of the ways that women, or young girls, learn to perceive their proper role within society and in the public school itself.

An additional point that receives a good deal less attention, even in the relatively innovative schools, is the causative connection between the rights of women in themselves (e.g., the ways that little girls relate to little boys right in the school) and the larger implications of political struggle on the part of women for the freedom of all people in conditions of oppression.

The problem that teachers face, in dealing with this issue, is how to speak of independent and irreverent women such as Dorothy Day, yet somehow manage to avoid dismissal or any of those other concomitant forms of vengeance that can be inflicted by a conservative and unforgiving school board. As in many other situations of this kind, teachers can often prove the point they need to make, yet simultaneously provide themselves with self-protection, just so long as they will choose, at least in the initial lessons, women who already have been canonized in public school but whose beliefs the children do not know and standard textbooks do not dare to tell. Out of a great many examples of such women, the one I find most vital, in the impact that her words can have, even on fifth-grade kids, is Helen Keller.

"Helen Keller," according to the standard text, "was a world-famous, deaf-blind lady who could read, write and speak."[11] The textbooks tell us also that she worked against "tremendous odds"—but with her, at all times, there stood "her trusted friend and teacher." Together, we learn, the two achieved things "all but past belief." Among the many famous people that she met were King George, Queen Mary, Lady Astor, Alexander Bell . . .

Most students encounter something similar to this at some point close to fifth or sixth grade. If, like many teachers, you have felt the sense of false narration I have just described, it might be of help to students to suggest this question: In the long run, does it matter a great deal how many famous people Helen Keller got to know? (Who really cares?) The one part of her work that seems to count the most is that she spent most of her life in fighting for the powerless and the poor.

"I have visited sweatshops, factories and crowded slums," she wrote. "If I could not see it, I could smell it. With my own hands, I could feel . . . dwarfed children tending their younger brothers and sisters while their mothers tended machines in nearby factories."[12]

She continues: "The foundation of society is laid upon a basis of . . . individualism, conquest and exploitation . . ." A social order such as this, "built upon such wrong [and] basic principles, is bound to retard the development of all."

The result, she says, is that the greed for money comes to be our major goal: "The output of a cotton mill or a coal mine is considered of greater importance than the production of healthy, happy-hearted and free human beings."

In regard to free elections, she has this to say: "We, the people, are not free. Our democracy is but a name. We vote? What does that mean? We choose between Tweedledum and Tweedledee."[13]

What would happen if a teacher were to put those words up on the wall under a photograph of Helen Keller? Or perhaps not the entire passage, but only the first line. "WE THE PEOPLE ARE NOT FREE."

To start with, it would certainly make a lot of people very angry. On the other hand, it's hard to know how teachers can be fired from a public school for putting up the words of Helen Keller on the wall. If the school system tried to fire a teacher on these grounds, they'd have a tough fight on their hands and, far more important from a pedagogic point of view, the public would receive a fascinating education.

Since the question will come up for sure, it seems important to establish here that all of these quotations come from the written works of Helen Keller. They come from either her speeches or her books. In order to make the basic point as powerful as we can, it might be of use to pose to students an explicit, loaded question of this kind: "How much of this material can you find—either in those books now present in the classrooms of the school or else in the school library? Do any of your textbooks offer even a little hint of these ideas?"

The follow-up question seems to be implicit: "If not, why not?" Obviously, the school officials know quite well that they might be in danger if their students start to hear the real ideas of some of those brave women who have fought so long and hard against injustice. Textbooks tell our students that Helen Keller learned to "see." They do not dare to tell them what she SAW. They tell our students that she learned to "speak," but do not dare to tell them what she SPOKE.

The textbooks are right, of course, that Helen Keller was a brave, heroic woman—but not for the reasons that the textbooks tell. She overcame at least two kinds of blindness: the blindness of the eyes (that blindness everybody knows) and then the blindness of the heart as well. Textbooks choose to talk about the first part only.

It is within our power to discuss the second, too.

6

The Hero in Jail:
"The Truth Will Make Us Free"

In trying to select historical examples of free-thinking men and women, teachers are forced to consider the question of their own protection in the face of potential critics on all sides. The ideal rebel, from a tactical point of view, is a person who has been already canonized by public school.

The area of black studies offers us an obvious example. I have always been fascinated by the life and work of Malcolm X. Nonetheless, in approaching the topic of racism with students, I think the words of Martin Luther King are bound to be much better starting points. They offer a conservative school board far less reason to give the teacher a hard time. King has already been credentialized by TV, press and public school—while Malcolm X has not. The point, however, once having made a tactical choice of biographical subject, is to refuse to accept the falsified version of Dr. King which school administrations will too frequently be asking us to sell.

Dr. King is regularly presented to our students as a noble, decent, but incredibly predictable and rather boring human being, who did a certain amount of "good" for his own people, adhered at all times to peaceful means, and never became impatient with white people.

Textbooks omit from the story of his life the only facts that make him genuinely great and worth our real respect. One of these facts, for instance, is that Dr. King, while peaceful in his tactics and devoted to the principles of Gandhi and Tolstoy, was nonetheless a militant and unyielding man who fought great battles and broke unjust laws, spent months in jail to dramatize the limits of conventional efforts carried out within the letter of the law—and urged the rest of us to find the willingness to do so also.

Dr. King spoke his mind freely, if perhaps somewhat too late, about the U.S. role in fostering needless and unjustifiable devastation in Vietnam and in other parts of Southeast Asia. He frequently expressed his outrage at the fact that Lyndon Johnson lied, first to the nation, then to the entire world, spoke of peace while dropping bombs on innocent civilians in Vietnam, leaving behind so many victims maimed, crippled or blind.

"America," said Dr. King, "is the greatest purveyor of violence in the world today." [14] He spoke these words on June 4, 1967. Ten months later, a sharpshooter in Memphis would prove his words correct by killing *him* as well. He was murdered on the terrace of a Memphis motel—a bullet fired through his throat.

Teachers can share with students the profound convictions that were honest reflections of the character of Dr. King, not the sanitized and prize-winning plastic preacher, but the man who spent so many days and nights in prison cells, lived with the constant threat of death and danger from the Ku Klux Klan, and also had to live with the blackmail of the F.B.I. Teachers can also extract, from straight respectable sources like *The Congressional Record* and *The Boston Globe,* a number of important stories on the ways that Dr. King was blackmailed by J. Edgar Hoover. [15]

None of this may please the local school board. As usual, however, the source of the material seems the key to our protection and survival. Any school that seeks to fire a teacher for the honest, undistorted use of documentation from the U.S. Senate and *The Boston Globe* is asking for considerable humiliation. In this way, teachers can with relative impunity make use of the life and words of Dr. King to pose some interesting questions to the students in their classes.

What is the reason for a man or woman to spend time in jail for his or her beliefs? What does it mean to be a "free" or "unfree" person in a nation that allows so little true and lasting freedom to its poorest citizens?

Are people free in any way that really counts if they are compelled to spend their lives within a prison made of lies? Dr. King once said that people who are not prepared to die for their beliefs aren't fit to live.[16] Teachers might provoke a startling debate even if they do nothing more than ask their students how they feel about such words. If the issue proves disturbing to the students, then the students might well bring it home to ask their parents, too.

Thoreau provides another dramatic example of a man who is included in the textbooks and curricula of public schools, but one who is denied most of those values and convictions that have given him a place in history. Ironically, with Thoreau, just as with Dr. King, the school boards have excluded from the acceptable life story virtually every item which compels them to include him in their textbooks in the first place. They are forced by his heroic and historic acts of civil disobedience to contain him in their province of consideration; but they are forced, by their alarm at this *same* power of disobedience, to delete or neutralize that very virtue. We might well wonder why they bother with him at all—if it were not for the obvious reply. They have to present him, respect him and defuse him, precisely in order that students will not meet him on their own. The dangers of disobedience, like those of sainthood, must be neutralized in warm, well-lighted rooms.

The purposes of the educational system would seem bizarre and self-defeating were they not so cleverly effective. It requires no conspiracy to bring about this intellectual emasculation. It is the natural behavior of well-educated and appropriately domesticated adults. All of us are complicit in these deeds, though many teachers have at last begun to learn the ways to free themselves from this complicity.

Like so many rebels of the past ten, twelve or fifteen years, Thoreau was thoroughly detested by a number of his fellow-citizens. Once he had been dead for many years, the schools and critics decreed that he had been a brilliant writer. It seems to be a rule of thumb in the United States, as in most other nations of the modern world, that the only acceptable rebel—certainly the one whose greatness is most certain and un-clouded—is a dead one.

If students could get an early look at some of the strongest political writings of Thoreau, they probably would find it much less difficult to understand why citizens of Massachusetts felt uneasy with his views. "How does it become a man to behave towards this American government today? I answer that he cannot without disgrace be associated with it." [17]

Thoreau was enraged by several attitudes and actions of the U.S. government, above all our toleration of the slave trade and the war with Mexico. Very few of the students that I meet in public schools today know anything at all about the war with Mexico. If they have even heard of it, I find it is the famous battles they remember. They do not remember either the purpose or the outcome. Few of them know that most of Arizona, all of California, Utah and Nevada, and a large part of Colorado and New Mexico, would not be parts of the United States at all if they had not been stolen wholesale by the U.S. Army. This, of course, is the real meaning of the war with Mexico.

One night, in 1846, Thoreau defied the U.S. government in the most dramatic way he knew. He spent a night in Concord jail as price of his refusal to pay taxes to support the Mexican war.

"When a sixth of the population of a nation which has un-dertaken to be the refuge of liberty are slaves, and a whole country [i.e., Mexico] is unjustly overrun and conquered by a foreign army and subjected to military law, I think that it is not too soon for honest men to rebel and revolutionize. . . . As for adopting the ways which the state has provided for dealing with the evil, I know not of such ways. They take too long and a man's life will be gone."

The heart of Thoreau's political opinion is contained within his essay *On the Duty of Civil Disobedience.* Curriculum guides generally make reference to this work but then divert our students to those sections of his longer books in which Thoreau speaks mainly about nature, woods and streams. These passages, of course, are beautiful and moving. This, however, is not the part of Thoreau's work that makes his name important in the history of ideas. Nor is it the part that renders him an influential moral force in almost every corner of the earth.

Teachers who care about Thoreau, and plan to speak of him at all, have it in their power to insist on going back to his essential work. School officials may perhaps inquire why it is that we do not restrict ourselves to his less controversial work—"the writing about nature."

Teachers can comfortably answer that it isn't writings about nature that have rendered Thoreau a central and seminal figure for so many of the world's nonviolent leaders. Why waste our students' time on aspects of the man that count the least?

I find that candid questions of that sort tend to disarm our interrogators. Many (hard as it may be for their potential victims to believe) have simply never thought of it before. Their tendency is less to be offended than bemused. It is experiences like these which lead me to withdraw my credence from various radical theories of "conspiracy." People pass on, often unknowingly, the lies their fathers and their mothers lived by. It seems to me that this statement comes much closer to the truth than any of the demonizing theories.

As in earlier chapters, what I am proposing here is the radical rediscovery of the innermost moral meanings of those heroines and heroes who have already been canonized by the public schools. Even when teachers choose their symbols and examples with great care, however, they still may be faced with serious trouble, inflicted by a hostile school board or a school official who is *not* "bemused" but, frankly, out to get them. It would be foolish, and misleading to young teachers, if I were to argue here that merely to invoke such names as Helen Keller and Thoreau and Dr. King, and then to defend them with a totally unexpected lack of guile, is going to serve as absolute protection against people who know very well exactly where their own self-interest lies and view our actions, therefore, as a threat.

Some administrators *are*, in truth, vindictive or afraid. Others are innocent of either malice or intelligence. And others still are highly intelligent, quietly grateful, and very much on our side. In this respect, as with most others raised within this book, there are, in short, no simple guarantees.

Postscript

Every distortion, every exclusion, every action of emasculation or denial of those men and women we have reason to revere, appears to find its curious counterpart in *another* body of American leaders who are clothed in the trappings of profundity and ethics which do not appropriately belong to them. While King is diminished, Lyndon Johnson is progressively transformed into an ardent activist for social justice. While Thoreau is appreciated as a sensitive man of nature, Emerson is exalted as the ethical and intellectual rebel he was not. While Garrison, Brown and Frederick Douglass are denied, and frequently forgotten altogether, Abraham Lincoln is given unwarranted praise and credit for the emancipation of the slaves.

The latter example is particularly disturbing to anyone who believes, as I do, that there are some genuine reasons to admire Lincoln. Abraham Lincoln was, unquestionably, one of our most distinguished presidents; we do not make him more distinguished, rather we tarnish him a bit, by attributing to him virtues he did not possess. The textbooks describe him as a "brave, heroic, kindly and generous man—famous, above all, as a fighter for the freedom of black people." The same books also speak of him as "Honest Abe." The second statement may very well be true. The first is not.

Lincoln signed the Emancipation Proclamation, as historians make clear, not because he was a partisan of equal privilege for all but—as ample evidence attests—because he was advised by friends that it would be to his political advantage to adopt this action. He did so, moreover, only after many years of desperate struggle by the real emancipators of black people. Those real emancipators of the blacks were, in large numbers, black themselves. Those who were not black were predominately the northern abolitionists. If it were not for the long and often dangerous struggle undertaken by these activists and constant agitators, Lincoln would not have been under pressure to emancipate black people.

This version of the truth is seldom stated in the books that school officials order for our classroom use. We can ascertain the truth, however, in any number of scholarly books which give an accurate history of the United States in the 1800s. Lincoln assigned to the black race a secondary role in our society. His attitude, indeed, is difficult to distinguish from that of the most committed segregationists of the 1980s. He did not simply *believe* that blacks deserved a separate and unequal role. He *said* so—and he did it in a speech which ought to be part of every U.S. text.

"I am not," he told his audience, "nor ever have been, in favor of bringing about in any way the social or political equality of the white and black races. . . . I will say in addition that there is a physical difference between the white and black races which, I suppose, will forever forbid the two races living together upon terms of social and political equality; and in as much as they cannot so live, that while they do remain together there must be a position of the superiors and the inferiors; and that I, as much as any other man, am in favor of the superior being assigned to the white man."[18]

Lincoln was, in many respects, an honest man. We should be honest, in turn, about *his* honesty. He was honest in describing his profoundly racist views. This is perhaps one reason why so many black men and women do not particularly like to see his photograph posted on the walls inside their schools.

We need to treasure the relatively small number of distinguished people who have risen to high office in our nation. One of the ways to do this, I believe, is to praise these people for their genuine and unquestioned virtues—while we concede, without a bit of hesitation, these prejudices, that narrowness of outlook, which they held in common with their generation. Lincoln will not appear to our students to be a lesser man for his deficiencies. He will appear to be more interesting, and more human, and more real—and therefore a person with whom both black and white kids can identify and grapple, or else struggle to confront.

The truth, here as in all ways, makes us free.

7

Secret Records

One of the most persistent instruments of class stratification, indoctrination and repression in the U.S. public schools is the "cumulative record." Academic, personal and psychological records of this nature exist for virtually all of the forty-three million students in our education system.[19] Much of the data in the cumulative record is of purely practical importance: height and weight, color of eyes, date of polio, typhoid and tetanus antitoxins, telephone number and address of parents. Other sections of the record are a lot *less* harmless and can frequently portend considerable danger to a student in the years ahead.

The sections which are probably most harmful are those that deal with reading scores, math levels, science aptitudes and other test results—especially those that have to do (or which are said to have to do) with matters such as I.Q. The latter items represent an area of ever-present danger to a student who has not succeeded in attracting the affection of his former teachers or his school administrators, but rather *has* succeeded in attracting their hostility and condemnation.

In many schools—especially in cases where, during the past ten years, there may have been racial tensions between teachers and the class—these folders often hold some truly painful commentaries. Often they are worded as advisories from one year's teacher to the next: "Benjamin is a potential rebel. Jennifer is very good at satirizing teachers. . . . Watch out for

Olivia and Susan. Either one can make the school day hopeless if she gets most of the children on her side . . ."

Few of the teachers who have entered public classrooms in the past few years have any reason to defend or justify these cumulative records. It is, indeed, their own suggestions and ideas that constitute the remainder of this chapter.

There is, first of all, a parallel to be drawn between the status of the students in battling against their lifelong supervision by the public schools and that of a very large number of adults in battling against surveillance by the government. Thousands of American citizens in the past five years have come to recognize the increasing dangers represented by the F.B.I., an agency set up initially (as we are told) for patriotic purposes, but used too often, in the years since 1965, to maintain records on political dissenters of all kinds. As we have seen, the former Director J. Edgar Hoover used the power of the F.B.I. not simply to gather documentation on important protest leaders but, in one notable case, in order to intimidate and blackmail Martin Luther King.

The cumulative folder is the school board's version of the secret records kept on citizens by the F.B.I. It holds the same potential danger for all students. That danger lies in one inevitable fact: It grants a great deal too much power to a small number of people to affect the present lives and future hopes of far too many. At its worst, it gives unscrupulous or misguided school officials (those who see a possible danger in a particular pupil's ethical intentions or political ideas) an almost limitless power to destroy that individual's career. Cumulative records have been used throughout the past ten years, for instance, to warn colleges, to which a student has applied, of possible threats that are implicit in the student's independent views.

The truth, too often, is that someone in the school administration does not *share* that student's views (or sometimes just dislikes him) and takes only enough data from his file to destroy his chances for admission to the college he is hoping to attend. Evidence shared with me in recent years confirms the fact that one of the nation's most prestigious universities has made occasional use of warnings of "potential rebels" during the process of selection, in order to be certain that the student body of the present period would be less troublesome and less political than the students of the 1960s and the early 1970s.

The consequence of political selection of this kind is bitterly frustrating: First the colleges learn the way to filter out potentially indignant or devoutly political applicants for entrance. Four years later, the press reports that "students on campus appear to be growing less political and more quiet and self-centered . . ." A carefully and methodically constructed lethargy is subsequently portrayed by gratified political leaders, careless sociologists and delighted college deans as if it were a curious but fortunate change of weather, perhaps "a cyclical phenomenon—ten years on and ten years off . . ." They describe as an objective phenomenon a situation which they have, themselves, unforgivably and in repeated breach of law and confidence, brought into being. Clearly, this is not the only reason for apparent quietude and student acquiescence in the academic world. Economic panic has a lot to do with it as well. So also does the media's distortion. But it is one obvious and initial cause.

Much of this would not happen, none of it could be done with so much ease, if it were not for the student dossiers provided by the cumulative records.

In view of the large number of cases of this kind, and especially in view of the well-noted fact that the right of access has already been won by adult citizens in coping with the records of the F.B.I., it seems to me a reasonable approach for teachers to initiate a similar policy of "open folders" with the pupils in their own class. Once a policy like this has been established, teachers in other classrooms will, of course, be far more careful as to what they dare to put into a cumulative folder in the first place. Once teachers know the folder will be read, not just by higher officials or by other teachers, but by the students too, those teachers will be a lot more cautious not to be sarcastic about someone that they simply do not like.

Even in schools and educational systems where opinion is divided, teachers at last are beginning to debate the pros and cons of open records with their students. Frequently, one of the other teachers in the school will grow uneasy, merely at the thought that students are even considering such issues, and especially under the aegis of another teacher in the school. Even those teachers who would, by personal preference, like to see an end to record-keeping of this kind cannot transcend an overriding fear that any rebellious action might be viewed as gross disloyalty by fellow educators.

There probably is no way to get around the fact that considerable anguish and a genuine "choice of sides" (on the part of teachers) are at stake. The truth is that—in good traditional terms—it *is* an act of breaking rank and taking sides with those (the pupils) who have often, in previous times, been viewed as adversaries by the staff. In terms of building teacher-pupil loyalty, however, it is an inescapable act. The price we pay is that some teachers may, at first, feel less at ease with certain colleagues than they did before. In the long run, I do not think that anyone we could possibly respect is going to suffer by reason of the fact that we are being honest with the pupils in our class. Among such teachers, I do not believe that a sense of tension or distrust is likely to persist for long. Soon enough, decent educators will discover that they have no reason for alarm. Those very few who do would not be valuable allies anyway.

The ideal resolution of the question—in all cases where this course of action is realistic, plausible and has some chance of amiable success—is first to discuss the matter with the principal and with all other teachers in the school, invite their willingness to rethink the whole issue about cumulative folders and, at the very least, to fight for a uniform respect for student privacy.

In such a way, the interests of the students are significantly advanced, if not yet totally protected, while the sense of solidarity among a good number of teachers will remain strong. Teachers who anticipate a lifetime of additional (and many more intimidating) struggles, will thereby have adhered to principle on the issue of the cumulative folder, yet they will have managed at the same time to maintain the loyalties of two groups—both students and their fellow teachers—who may be of strength and help to them in years ahead.

There is another solution which some schools have seized upon—but it is neither an honest nor attractive one. It is to keep two *complete sets of records for each pupil.* One set is relatively harmless and routine and remains, therefore, within the teacher's desk or filing drawer. The other one is not routine at all. It contains all sorts of personal and subjective comments, along with I.Q. scores, predictive opinions from psychologists and such—and stays, therefore, within the principal's locked files. Parents and students who do not know of the existence of a second set of files will not, of course, have any way to ask to see its contents. Only a helpful friend within the system—the student's teacher, for example—has a chance to help those students and their parents to discover all the things they have a right to know.

School boards cannot easily—or legally—suspend us or dismiss us for an action of this kind. Parents and children now have theoretical right of access to virtually all records in every state and city in the nation.[20] Clearly, however, school administrations have other ways than those which are official to retaliate against a teacher for his or her behavior or beliefs. If we have already done some work to build a groundwork of strong loyalties and friendships with the parents and their children, then principals and school boards will at least think twice before they try to use such methods of revenge.[*]

Much of my emphasis, up to now, has been upon the ways in which we might be able to maintain the loyalties of teachers, yet at the same time build a sense of solidarity with the students in the school. As the efforts we make to stand up for the rights of students grow more serious and sustained, it seems almost inevitable that some of our fellow teachers will begin to draw away from us—if not for good, at least for a limited period of time.

In the past year, in the course of a seminar that I did with classroom teachers, many of the teachers would reiterate the point that, sooner or later, you could not be loyal to your conscience, loyal to your students, open with their parents, and still remain totally trusted and accepted by all of the other teachers in the school. I am sure that this is true; yet I also believe that really good teachers will continue to remain our friends and allies in these difficult situations, just so long as it is clear that our behavior is entirely conscientious and responsible.

Malicious teachers who attempt to curry favor among students and their parents out of a quiet sense of satisfaction or delight at the power to subvert the lives of others often end up losing everybody's trust.

Immature teachers sometimes fall into this trap; but these are not the kinds of rebel teachers who will change the public schools. A gentle rebel often moves more slowly, agrees to bypass some of the small battles, tries very hard to avoid the needless suffering of others—and ends up winning the real war. This is the kind of ally we can only hope for.

---

[*] The Family Education Rights and Privacy Act, also known as the Buckley Amendment (1974), would appear to provide an absolute resolution of this problem if it could be conscientiously and consistently enforced. Unhappily, for the sake of many children, this is—as of the present writing—not the case. (See note 20 on p. 175.)

8

"Lead Children to the Following Six Points..."

Those who do not know the inner mysteries of public school may not be familiar with a curious classroom institution known as the "teacher's guide."

A teacher's guide provides instructions for the teacher as to certain methods guaranteed to help us lead our students to a set of seemingly inevitable conclusions, yet simultaneously to get the students to believe that it is *they* who have arrived at these conclusions on their own. There is a separate guide for each commercial line of standard texts. The publisher prepares the guide as one of the means by which to win the teacher, or school system, to the newest history, math, geography or English series.

The guide appears to serve two obvious objectives:

(1) to help the teacher put across the lessons without needing to devote a vast amount of time to preparation;

(2) to render the teacher something of a captive to a single series. Unfortunately, while seeming to make the teacher's job more simple, the teacher's guides are also taking away the satisfaction of all independent and creative labor in the preparation of the daily work. The guidebook seems to be the teacher's friend. Insidiously, it also robs the teacher of the only intellectual dignity which our profession still allows us: the individual, passionate or whimsical exhilaration of *invention*. We cease to be the

architects even of one reading period each morning—or of one English lesson every afternoon.

We obtain a set of neat, swift, "classroom-tested" lesson plans to sell these mediocre texts to children. The guidebook sells the series to the teacher, and the teacher sells the textbook to the class: a progression of increasingly well-planned seductions. In the end, we are the pitiful addicts of the little red annotations printed in the margins of our book, suggested by an invisible expert in a distant city. The expert is rarely a person we recognize by reputation. The preparation of these guidebooks is the special province of the second-rate and the seldom seen.

But this is only a small part of the problem: the insult to the teacher. There is, above all, the insult—and the injury—to our students. I have joined with other teachers in long and exhaustive studies of these guidebooks in the past five years. Some of the more obnoxious are published and distributed by the massive textbook factory, Scott Foresman, a company which is sufficiently adaptable to its potential market to have distributed two parallel editions at the time that I was teaching school: one with multiracial illustrations, one with no black people in the book at all. I am told that the latter edition has since been phased out of existence.

Most of the guidebooks offer confident predictions on the way that students will react (or "ought to") in the face of certain stories, poems, ideas. ("Children can be easily led to recognize and understand the special beauty of the image *heart like cracked gravel,* line six, stanza three. Point out, if the opportunity occurs, that this is a simile.")

The passage above does not do serious damage to a student's heart and mind. It falls into the category, rather, of a foolish, somewhat boring and dishonest waste of time. (What if a student happens to be bright enough to understand, for instance, that this is not a "beautiful image" after all, but an impossible image in a very, very sorrowful piece of verse?) The guidebooks that are truly dangerous, however, are those which try to tell us how to lead a class of students to a "logical" conclusion in the areas of politics and current issues. Most of these logical conclusions, as we know too well, have to do with jingoistic loyalties, the recognition of the merits of the U.S. economic system, and the power, prestige and importance of the United States as compared to those of nations which adhere to socialist ideals.

Many teachers no longer will deny their own intelligence and taste by using books like these. Others, however, find themselves in situations where they have no choice. Either they use the guidebook and make lesson plans according to the rules, or else they risk the likelihood of condemnation by their supervisors, charges of stubborn and recalcitrant behavior leading at last either to demotion or else to suspension or expulsion. Imaginative teachers who are in this situation, and who clearly recognize the devious behavior in which they are invited to participate, now and then have used their ingenuity and skill in order to arrive at a way out. In fewest words, what they have managed to achieve is to make certain that the guidebook cannot lead their students to those preplanned conclusions at which its authors confidently predict they will "arrive." In order to do this, teachers simply figure out a tactful way to get a copy of the guidebook into the hands of children.

School officials who hear of this may well condemn our action as the very essence of unprofessional behavior. Teachers, however, seem to be on solid ground with the straightforward answer that their students have a very high stake in recognition of the details of the way by which the process of indoctrination works.

Obviously, teachers are likely to run into a good deal less resistance if they are able to address potential critics in a noncombative tone which more or less anticipates agreement. The manner of the teacher is, more often than not, the crucial factor in obtaining a satisfactory outcome to these altercations.

The assumption of a hostile answer can pretty well guarantee that we will come across as adversaries in the eyes of our superiors. On the other hand, a gentle sense of "presupposed agreement among sensitive co-workers" is a very appealing way to cope with those whom we are eager to win over. It is my own misfortune that I was often, in my first year as a teacher, more eager to "take a stand" than to achieve a goal. If the objective is to demythologize some of the worst of these expensive texts and readers, it does not help to let our principal believe we view him as a fool.

Once students have had a chance to see one of these teacher's guides, they frequently will ask their teacher how to get their hands on multiple copies of the book. One teacher in Nebraska told me that she sends these students to the principal. If the principal answers that he has no power to consent, the teacher sends them to the school committee. It is hard to see how school committees can refuse a student who requests the right to buy one of these books. If the school committee does refuse, however, it is simple enough for us to tell our students how to write off to the publisher and order a few of these documents themselves. (We can, of course, always lend them several copies of our own.) Once they have a couple of guidebooks in their own possession, it is an easy matter to assist them in examination of particular pages, then Xerox and distribute copies to their classmates.

Sometimes, as with guidebooks for the literature texts, the consequence is merely comical. In other subject areas such as history and government, the end results are genuinely explosive. It isn't pleasant to discover that a book, or a school system, that appears to have been urging you to think, reflect and shape your own view of the world, is, in fact, by clear intention, leading you by clever stages to a set of inescapable conclusions. It is even more unpleasant when these logical conclusions manage, almost every time, to demonstrate the failure—or, more tastefully stated, "the disappointing aspects"—of all other ways of life, in contrast, of course, to the way that we live here in the United States.

The various approaches that I have suggested here, relatively gentle in their flavor and quite certainly within the limits of the law, have nonetheless led, in several cases, to intense reactions on the part of students. A teacher's guide appears to be about as dull and nonsubversive as the stories of George Washington and Betsy Ross. Yet, turned around for uses such as those I have proposed, it can be a quite effective means by which to undercut at least one instrument of student indoctrination and control.

The knowledge that a class of students has been able to examine various sections of the teacher's guide, even before a teacher has had the chance to put those sections into use, will sometimes cause a certain amount of anguish in some of the other teachers in the school. It is like the issue of the cumulative folders. For most teachers, however, this is not the case at all. Teachers are by no means such predictable and uniform cowards as the public likes to think. Many teachers, frankly, find the revelation (to their pupils) of the teacher's guide, and similar manipulative materials, a great source of relief. Very few teachers get much satisfaction out of doing lessons where they know that they will have no possible chance of learning something new, because they are advised well in advance exactly what the class is going to "ask"—and also what the class is going to "discover."

Teachers, for decades, have been denied, thereby, not only the satisfaction of creative and imaginative planning of their own day's labor but also almost every opportunity for intellectual discovery, surprise—the unexpected. They write down in advance, on Sunday afternoons, in lesson books, the tedious ideas their students will discover Wednesday mornings in their English or their social studies class.

The tragedy in all of this is twofold.

The teacher's professional value is reduced, by the foregoing process, to that of a technical go-between. In political respects, the teacher is reduced to pimping for the textbook authors—those, in turn, who have already offered the little talent they possess to satisfy the political intentions of the powers that be.

I once looked over a teacher's guide in California which gave the teacher of social studies the following directions: "Lead students, by free and open discussion, to the following six reasons for the failure of socialism in Red China . . ."

The wording reflects the knee-jerk acquiescence of the textbook writers to the current political jargon of the nation. A decade later, they would not have said "Red China." Ever since Richard Nixon set foot on the tarmac in Shanghai, China has come to be labeled by its real name. Today, the very same teacher's guide, in search of suitable demons, would doubtless shift its animus to another Marxist nation. There, too, our students would be led to discover the seven, eight—or eighteen—reasons for the failure of an ideological system that our government views with disapproval.

The pejorative adjective, however, represents the least of evils. It is the manipulative teaching process which degrades the teacher most. What do we do with the disagreeable child who *refuses* to discover "the six reasons"? What of the child, for example, who comes up with only four or who insists that there are only three? What of the unhappy child, for that matter, who decides, by some calamitous mistake, that socialism is not failing in "Red China" after all?

The student who breaks the predictive pattern that has been laid out for the teacher who must use the teacher's guide becomes all at once a positive threat to the uninterrupted presentation of the daily lesson. The teacher, having once subscribed to this inane procedure, is left in an unenviable position. The uncooperative student becomes an adversary of that teacher, even indeed of the teacher who never believed in the procedure in the first place. The teacher's guide has erected a wall between the teacher and the student—perhaps the very student who was most likely to have given the class a moment of the unexpected.

One of the greatest satisfactions of teaching, in my own belief, is the ever-present possibility of "taking the imagination by surprise"—our own imagination or that of the children in our midst. Once we consent to conduct our class in accordance with the orders of Scott Foresman, we forfeit entirely the gratification of being taken by surprise. It is one of those factors that contributes rapidly to teacher burn-out, to tedium, to weariness, to a loss of day-to-day exhilaration.

Equally disheartening is the loss of anything that resembles dialogue between the teacher and the class. There cannot be dialogue in a situation that has been so carefully stage-managed. At best, one achieves the bizarre phenomenon of "divided monologue." The teacher asks, and the teacher replies— even though the replies appear to be coming from the mouths of children. In reality, the script that has been provided by the guidebook, adapted perhaps by the teacher who prepared the lesson plan, is subsequently read in two-part harmony by the teacher and the class. *It is all, however, being spoken by one person.*

A preplanned nationally standardized monologue disguises itself as the dialogue of authentic education. It is an offense against all parties who must play the game; but the offense is greatest against the one who knows that the outcome has been "fixed" and still must play it with a smile. It is no wonder, then, that so many teachers either disregard these standard readers and their guidebooks altogether or else resort to such methods of subversion as the one I have proposed.

Once our students have a copy, or at least some sections, of the teacher's guide right on their desks, we find all at once that the use of that guide begins to serve a totally new function. Instead of the skilled manipulation of the students to arrive at predetermined places, it allows teachers and students together to study the very process of manipulation. A method intended to be used in service of aesthetic or ideological control serves us instead as a means of tearing the wrappings from the system altogether. The teacher's guide becomes the object of an "ideological dig." Teacher and pupil, like eager anthropologists, interpret a strange society (that of the public school) by close examination of a precious, whole, undamaged piece of clay. Humor abounds—but so, too, do ethical uproar and enlightened scrutiny. The sense of relief for many teachers is, if possible, even greater than that which will be afforded to their students.

In spite of all that I have said above, many teachers who have been using books like these for several years are going to feel threatened. Those who are least willing to smile at some of the absurdities with which we have, for too long, been obliged to live may even attempt to charge us with disloyalty.

If this should happen, although it does mean trouble for somebody (or, at very least, bad feelings), it can also spark some fascinating and unprecedented class discussions, as well as some helpful discussions among teachers, on the ethics of the whole idea of standardized deception in the public schools. Certainly, between the textbook publisher, school board and the class, there *has* been very serious and real deception.

The question is this: Which of the three—school board, publisher or students—should we call dishonest?

9

History from the Bottom Up

As we have seen, the child who dares to criticize the books provided by the public school can often expect to hear a certain familiar and predictable reply: "If you don't like this book that we gave you, let's see if you can write a better one yourself."

In the past few years, a number of teachers have had the sense of mischief and imagination to take up this challenge—but to turn it around in ways most principals and school boards don't expect.

In itself, a student-written text is nothing new. It is something that's been done before, but generally only in a time of crisis and also most frequently in a manner that did not distinguish it greatly from the textbooks that we had already. The content was better; but the format was pretty much unchanged. Civil rights workers in the 1960s put together something of this sort for students in the hundreds of "Freedom Schools" that were begun in Georgia, Alabama, Mississippi. It was a book for teaching kids to read—not by telling tales of Dick and Jane, but by direct use of the stories of the struggles and rebellions of black people. Its title, not surprisingly, was *The Freedom Reader*. Labor union organizers have also done counter-textbooks of their own for many years. More recently, a group of high school students in Wisconsin have begun to work on a similar idea.

Teachers who intend to set out with their students on a project of this sort sometimes find it helpful to examine first the special categories of distortion that seem to be predominant within the standard texts. It isn't just the obvious lies that publishers put *in,* but also the essential truths which they leave *out,* that constitute the ultimate deception. The point, then, is to do a lot more than to fix that which is present. The point is also to replace what has been lost.

History, as students almost always learn it, is not really history at all. It is the history of privilege, the history of those who have the power, cash and pleasure, not of those who do the work, who undergo the hardship and absorb the blows. In many cases, history—as it is made available in public school—is not a great deal more than endless tabulations of the actions and the attitudes of famous people: kings and commissars, builders and brokers, bankers, scientists, artists, authors and inventors, sometimes conquerors and killers.

Narratives of war are almost always stories of the bold and clever tactical ideas of generals and admirals. Seldom do we read about the lives and deaths of twenty million soldiers in the front lines. "International relations," by the same evasion, have always been described as confrontations and negotiations by the rulers or the representatives of rulers (such people as Von Ribbentrop, Molotov, John Foster Dulles), seldom as the lives and struggles undergone by those nine hundred million human beings who were organizers, soldiers, carpenters, coal carriers, day laborers—or children and school teachers—within the nations which these men controlled. U.S. history, too many times, is little more than rather dry, uninteresting and repetitive descriptions of quadrennial elections, followed by the so-called "Major Contributions" of each president, no matter how unoriginal, dishonest or inept.

As an initial act of independence, therefore, many of the student textbook writers reject for good those four-year spans that separate elections. By this decision, they subvert, right from the start, the semblance of importance which is otherwise assigned to those unreal and insubstantial choices between two affluent candidates—or those who have been hand-picked by the affluent—then to be sold as plausible and legitimate alternatives to a public which has had no input from the start. (Even the outcome of a primary election is determined by the campaign staff and budget of the candidate with the largest bank account.) The students win themselves, at the same time, a lot of space in which to speak of people and events that seem to them to count a great deal more: to draw, for instance, on the voices of those people whom the scholars used to call "the silent poor." Thus, from the start, they are prepared to tell these tales not from the "top" down but from the "bottom" up.

History not of a heroic westward drive on part of the United States, but history as murder and exploitation of the only native residents of North America.

History not of Waltham watches, but of Waltham women, history also of the international workers of the world, of the steel, coal, railroad workers' union, of the International Ladies' Garment Workers' Union.

History not of well-paid generals and their heroic deeds, but history of the frontline soldiers who lay down their lives in battle while the generals held expensive banquets at headquarters.

History of transportation, medicine and law, not in terms of high-speed turbotrains, of "milestone" decisions in the federal courts, epoch-making "breakthroughs" in the clinics of the rich, but documentation of high ghetto death rates, overcrowded clinics in Los Angeles, Chicago, the South Bronx.

History of legal process as dispensed not by distinguished jurists on the federal bench, but by the circuit judges of the Alabama courts. Travel not by Eastern Airlines but by Greyhound, Trailways and by thumb. History of business, profit and production not in terms of handsome photographs of Andrew Carnegie, John Rockefeller, Henry Ford, but industry in terms of labor, cash and its real sources: where it comes from, who creates it, who possesses it and who enjoys it.

The challenge here is not just one of refutation of a history of lies. It is a matter also of the textbook's point of observation—or, as photographers say, "the angle of vision." Even the most innovative texts of recent years speak of slave days still from the untroubled point of view of those who were *not* slaves but were either southern scholars or else northern commentators. Unjust customs viewed from universities, from libraries or from the hotel balconies of those who were their instigators, planners, profiteers, cannot be described in voices of necessity, of urgency and rage—but only, at the best, of kindliness, of pity, of amelioration. (A few books have been published in the past ten years which constitute significant exceptions; but all of these books are highly selective in their subject area—and these are not the books, in any case, that are selected or "adopted" by the public schools.)

History, as taught in public school, is history as seen from the top down. It is history as ordinary people would not feel it, did not live it and would not describe it. This is all the greater reason, then, why teachers who intend to help their students in the composition and production of a truly interesting book need to do an awful lot of work to help those students find the voices, documents and stories of the struggles of the poor.

One of the most obvious ways to help to free our students from the limitations of the textbooks and encyclopedias which are already on the shelf is by urging them to make use of a major library. If our students don't have time or travel money to do research of this kind, older friends in nearby universities will often do it for them. If they can't, the list of leads in the back section of this book ought to be of use in helping students to discover and obtain a lot of rich and interesting information on their own.

If the student-written text is to go beyond the stories about generals and millionaires and queens and kings, teachers have to help their students, in one way or other, to discover and record the voices of the common men and women who reflect the real life out of which all history is made. This is especially the case in writing about minorities, as well as about women. Our tendency is to attempt to make up for the errors of the past by listing (and praising) as many notable blacks, or women, as we can possibly "collect"—in order, it seems, to struggle back *in kind* against all of those white male Anglo-Saxon figures who now dominate the school curricula. We continue, however, to write about important people, prize-winning people, blacks of grandeur, women of great fire, fame or wit. We do not write about ordinary people.

For women especially, an authentic reclamation of history seems to demand that we examine those who worked in the sweatshops, those who were the backbone of the cottage industries, those who were midwives and ran schools for *other* midwives, those who operated little-known (and once-forbidden) "underground schools" for runaway slaves during the 1800s.

These are not women who were invited to the White House, led massive protest movements or delivered fiery, famous and exciting speeches. They are the women, however, without whom none of their leaders would have come to our attention because they would not have had anyone to lead. Their lives and words are an elemental part of what I mean by history "from the bottom up." I do not mean "bottom" in a condescending way—like "pitiful but decent." I mean those women who were workers, farmers, fighters, organizers and front-runners in the struggles of their times. Many of those elderly men and women still alive today can tell the stories of their mothers and grandmothers. Students can record and then transcribe and edit stories of this kind.

Another early stage within the struggle to demystify the standard texts is to involve our pupils in a close examination of the *language* that is used in many of these books, in order to begin to understand the power of a loaded word or phrase. Once students start to recognize the way that traditional textbooks load their words, then they can begin to figure out the way to do it on their own—but from a different point of view.

Teachers must often go to some extremes to demonstrate to students that there is no way to write "unloaded" language. Every word conveys some kind of bias, even if it is just the bias of those people who have given up so much of their own selves that they no longer have strong feelings about anything. (Theirs is the bias of surrender.) If students in the class wish to dispute this point, it might be of interest to invite them to attempt to make a statement in the subject area of politics or social change which is not loaded in one way or other.

An obvious example of a loaded word—one which was discussed, in passing, earlier in this book—is the modifier *radical*. The adjective is used in school as if it were a dangerous deviation from a healthy modifier: *liberal*. It is within the power of the students, if they so desire, to turn this right around. I have heard at least one high school teacher, obviously a little more audacious than most others, who spoke of liberals as "people who say that they agree with things the radicals have done—but don't intend to do those things themselves."

As we have seen, there are many teachers who do not choose to talk in terms like these. Teachers who hesitate to talk too much in class, but recognize that they cannot help but demonstrate a bias anyway, often try to work around their hesitation by resorting to a method that I have described above: setting out a broad, diverse, but still (inevitably) weighted set of offerings—both ideological and historical materials—a selection which will elicit many of the issues that are being mentioned here. Other teachers see no reason why they should not speak out bluntly for themselves. I see no reason why a teacher needs to "choose," or why we ought not to invite (and to expect) a mixture of both methods. The point, in either case, is to bestir the minds of students to perceive large areas of possible distortion and deception in familiar language use which they have not previously considered, and would have no opportunity to think of, without lots of outside help.

The same teacher I quoted above speaks to his class in terms somewhat like these: "Again and again, in history, whenever crisis comes, you'll find that liberals tend to turn against their former radical co-workers." If the students doubt this (as many do), he says: "Why don't you do some research and find out? Look a little into liberal behavior inside Germany during Hitler's rise to power."

If the students still feel skeptical, then he suggests they do the same thing also in regard to liberal behavior here in the United States during the time that Joe McCarthy came to power. "Several prominent newsmen that you hear today on national TV turned in their radical friends to save their jobs." After a sharp, non-neutral, controversial statement of that kind, the class at least has something of real interest to debate. Whatever the repercussions, class discussion won't be dull.

Another first step for a class that plans to write a counter-textbook of its own is to examine not only lies, omissions, loaded words, but format also—the entire manner of presentation of familiar texts. Most students are so well trained, for instance, to the use of sections and divisions, "units" and "sub-units," that it begins to be extremely hard to figure out the way to bypass all this complicated scaffold. Some of the structure of a standard textbook is, I suppose, essential. Most often it's of use to print an index. It also makes some sense to publish footnotes, especially in order to protect the class against the charge of reckless, overstated views. These, however, are quite different matters from the "units" and "sub-units" of the standard text.

Teachers can open up this issue with their students in a pretty direct and uninhibited way. (There's nothing about the subject which should threaten anyone in public school or in the F.B.I.) We ought to let our students know that they don't need to lock up all of their best ideas in boxes and containers. We ought to let them know that items can drift—and sometimes overlap. We ought to let them know they can repeat a point that seems important ten or fifteen times—maybe only for the sake of causing us to wonder why. We ought to let them know they do not need to print an illustration every two and a half pages. They might allow five pages with *no* illustrations—then, all at once, explode with fold-out photos, cartoons and other designs.

All of the above is based upon the supposition that the class and teacher have in mind the composition only of a single text. There is no reason why this need be so. Hundreds of other variations come to mind: multiple books on separate topics, for example, radical comic books for students of younger ages than those in your class, books on HOW TO WRITE A BOOK FROM SCRATCH, books which aim exclusively at local issues, books which do not try to match the national appeal of standard texts but which instead are aimed at one place and one season only.

One final thought: A lot of students, even in the preparation of their own text, hesitate to advertise their own beliefs in clear and passionate words. This inhibition is a natural carry-over from the inhibitions which so many of their teachers feel as well. Other students, however, have been able to get past this hesitation. They flood their work with totally wide-open statements (sometimes bitter, sometimes biting and sometimes satiric) of their own point of view. They also advertise the bias of their views by two-inch titles or by comical and unconventional headlines.

The sole purpose of such headlines is to challenge, sidestep, and even satirize, the standard textbook pretense of a neutral point of view. Thus, if another teacher looks at what the class has done and tells the students that it seems to tell "only one side," they can be candid and can answer that he or she is absolutely right. Those who wish can get the other side from TV, from the press or from the texts that still are lined against the wall. Honest bias is the best defense against such accusations later on.

"Of course it tells our side. That's why we wrote it."

10

Issues That Start to Send Our Students Home in Tears

Each example I have given, in the last three sections, remains within the precincts of the school itself: cumulative records, teacher's guides and student-written texts. The idea of action, growing out of a period of reflection, becomes a great deal more exciting and a whole lot more important when the process leads both class and teacher outside of the school into the world beyond.

It is one thing, however, to encourage students to take action on their own beliefs. It is quite another to encourage our pupils to go out and to take action on those ethical convictions which we have identified already as our own. It would, no doubt, be far less troublesome for teachers if we could feel content to state no more than this: "Students should be faithful to their own intense beliefs and feel the power to turn ethical intentions into lived convictions." It *would* be more convenient, but it would be totally dishonest.

The truth is that teachers do not think of "lived conviction" as an abstract virtue, but rather of conviction in the context of particular moral mandates and specific human needs. Many are needs and mandates that are likely to disturb our students and, perhaps, create in them a state of ethical upheaval that might sometimes send them home in fury or in tears. Whenever this happens, teachers need to be prepared for parent complaints, neighborhood concern and heightened anxiety levels within the administration of the school.

On the other hand, if teachers have engaged in prior and extensive groundwork with the parents of the pupils (groundwork of the kind that will be indicated in the second section of this book), then I think that it is worth the risk to raise such issues in the presence of the class, and I suspect that many of our principals and fellow teachers will support us. There are, certainly, large numbers of unfrightened educators who have been introducing issues of considerable provocation into public schools and urging their students to "get up and do something about it"—yet do not appear to have been beaten down by critics from inside or from outside of the schools.

One of the most familiar objections that is likely to occur is the question of the wisdom of creating "dangerous guilt feelings" in young people. A conventional viewpoint that repeatedly appears to win support from conventional physicians —especially conventional psychiatrists—advises us that all straightforward guilt, undecorated conscience and bad dreams are both unsound and (probably) symptoms of neurosis. The teacher who inspires such uncomfortable feelings is, of course, regarded by the social system as the most neurotic one of all.

The sinister part of all of this, of course—and certainly, in long-range terms, the most alarming—is that our logic rapidly leads us very quickly to believe that there are not *some* situations to which guilt might well be the only sane response. It also leads us to forget the sane and practical distinction to be drawn between two very different kinds of guilt which share, unfortunately, a single name: the guilt that simply binds up individuals within a tight and frightened knot of shame and fear, and—in striking contrast—that experience of pain and outrage, followed by a sense of individual self-liberation, which functions not as a neurotic bind but rather as a threshold into energetic and reflective action. It is a feeling which does not act to constrain but proves, rather, catalytic in its power to provoke us to enormous personal growth and new perceptions.

Of all potentially disturbing issues (those which might indeed be threatening to the children of rich people) the one most painful is the question of our own responsibility for the physical and psychological ordeal of those who live in our own social system but whose existence we are somehow able to perceive as disconnected from our own.

Many times students will begin, in class discussions on this subject, by taking an exceedingly defensive stand: "What does the life or death of children in the South Bronx have to do with you or me?" If they sit and talk a while longer with their teachers, it might become uncomfortably clear exactly what it has to do with all of us.

The children of white landlords who own rental units in a nearby urban slum often live well, eat good food and attend superior schools, at the direct expense of very poor people who live in neglected and unwholesome tenements which have been rented to them by *our* parents. The children of prosperous doctors in the northern cities often can afford to wear expensive clothes, travel to Europe in the summer, practice their tennis in exclusive clubs, because their fathers or mothers choose to care for people who can pay them high fees, leaving poor people—largely blacks and Spanish-speaking—to wait in line at poorly staffed health clinics where medical care is marginal at best. The children of rich, sometimes aristocratic owners of large farms and cattle ranches often live in pleasant, rich and elegant homes because their fathers hire, at low wages, illiterate farm workers, offer them no health protection, house them in filthy overcrowded shacks and make no effort to provide them with that bit of education that might lead them to protest against such desperate conditions.

All prosperous white students aren't the children of rich doctors, avaricious lawyers, predatory slumlords. Nor are all white middle-class young people really "prosperous" at all. (Many, although we think of them as middle class, often live in economic hardship which the national statistics do not honestly reflect.) It seems important to emphasize this point because I do not like to reinforce the crippling and simplistic view that every student whom we teach in school is either a victim or else the victimizer. Millions of students live in something of an economic limbo. Nonetheless, for a very large number of the affluent students in our schools, pleasure and well-being *are* obtained, in large degree, at the direct expense of many millions of others who live very close to the survival margin. It is this relatively privileged group that I now have in mind.

Once children from this background start to talk and think of poverty and excess in the meticulous way that I propose, and with the conscious and unhesitant participation of their teachers, they rapidly discover that there *are* some real and obvious connections between their own lives and those of the very poor people with whom they might already identify and with whom they sometimes even work as volunteers, but up to now only in a charitable or paternalistic state of mind. All at once, an unanticipated factor enters their consideration. It is not just that some folks have a little—and some others have a lot. One thing, rather *depends* upon the other.

Textbook publishers do their best to dodge this possibility altogether. They try very hard to choose a type of language that will manage to obscure the whole idea of causes and connections between rich and poor. School books seldom use a gritty word like *exploitation* or *oppression*. Instead, in writing of black people, for example, they speak in terms of *deprivation*. Deprivation sounds like something that "just happens" (a thunderstorm, a case of hiccoughs or the flu), rather than something that one person does to someone else. "Too little" can be said (about one social class)—but not "too much" (about the other). To say "too little" and "too much" in the same sentence is to make clear that we live, not simply in a land of pain, but also in a nation of injustice.

Troublesome or not, this is a subject which an earnest and

persistent teacher cannot easily pass by. Exploitation is not carried out by no one, but by someone. That someone—doctor, landlord, or landowner—no matter how careful we may try to be, is going to prove to be somebody's rich father. If we teach in an especially rich neighborhood, or even just a well-off neighborhood, there is an excellent chance that many of the children whom we teach are rich because some other folks are poor.

To deal with matters that come so close to home is not an easy business—especially for a teacher who has warm and affectionate feelings for the pupils in his class. It often means anger. Sometimes it means tears. There is no way, however, by which teachers of privileged children can avoid this point if we believe those children should receive the chance to grow up, not just smart and slick, but also ethical and strong.

If the teacher needs to postpone matters of this sort on tactical grounds—if the teacher, for instance, has good reason to anticipate a far more serious confrontation later on, perhaps with conservative groups that have already made it clear that they are watching his behavior—that is an unassailable reason to move gently in the area I have suggested. If, on the other hand, a teacher chooses to step back from any discussion of the causative connections which make poverty a fact of life in the United States, and if that teacher's only reason is a hesitation to face up to repercussions of his own beliefs, then I should think that teacher would perceive himself as working in collusion with the lies the textbooks teach. I cannot imagine any other way that we could understand such hesitation.

It is probably correct that teachers cannot easily raise these issues with the pupils of the first or second grade. On the other hand, from fifth or sixth grade on, it is difficult to justify a teacher's circumvention of these basic truths. It would be a relief to me, as to most teachers, if we could somehow always find a reason to sidestep these difficult dilemmas. I don't think that we *can,* however; and I don't think that we *should.*

In every neighborhood, in almost every generation, certain privileged children of the affluent members of society do find the courage to break away from many traditional ideas in order to work instead beside the victims of their social order. To make that choice, as many teachers know from their own life and work, is very hard. There is no reason, therefore, why students ought to suffer twice: once for sadness at the loss of all those things that once were easy and familiar, then a second time for guilt at being born the children of rich people.

If some of our students honestly should resolve to take a stand beside a victimized minority, they may not leave their homes in any drastic physical respect. In moral terms, however, they do make the choice to take sides with the victims of a world their folks, with rare exceptions, have either helped to shape or, at the least, accepted without protest. Students who come to this decision often suffer deeply for the distance it creates between themselves and their old friends and other teachers.

If students start to learn of pain and exploitation in their midst, their city, state or nation, and if they choose to disregard that pain (as many normal people do), then they have reason to feel guilty. If, however, they have begun to act upon their sense of what is just and true, and then have taken sides as well, and put their energies to work for weeks on end within a day-care center, or a clinic, or learned how to churn out leaflets from a ditto master for a strong street organization (like those many groups which do in fact exist throughout the country), then I see no reason why—from that point on—they ought to live with either guilt or any other form of inappropriate self-accusation.

In dealing with this issue, unlike many others treated in this book, it seems self-evident that there is only modest value in the act of exhortation in itself, since even the most ardent words of teachers still remain within the inert limitations that contain almost all other processes of public education. Only the teacher's actual participation in specific actions of his or her own personal determination (in keeping with those values that the teacher, and not necessarily the teacher's pupils, might hold dear) is likely to establish a persuasive precedent for pupils to take independent action of their own.

It is, of course, all the more exciting—and more deeply moving to everyone concerned—if, at some stage, the teacher's struggle and that of the pupils should turn out to be the same.

Postscript

I have distinguished in these chapters between two different kinds of guilt. Many students find themselves caught up in a neurotic and entangling labyrinth of self-accusation. Others are able to move forward from this state of mind into a vigorous process of self-liberation.

One of the ways by which the teacher can assist a student who is caught up in the former state of mind is to attempt to help to break down large and overwhelming socioeconomic problems into manageable items which are small enough for students first to pinpoint, then to attack head-on. So long as a problem appears to be too grandiose to be approached by ordinary, isolated and youthful human beings, students respond by stepping away and giving up the effort altogether: "The problem is too big."

I do not propose that we ignore realistic recognition of those many surrounding forces that control the schools, the banks, the neighborhoods, the hospitals or the police. I do suggest, however, that each teacher and each student need to find the willingness to enter into piecemeal battle, even in the face of larger issues, of whatever shape or size.

Struggles that we and our students hope to undertake ought to be measured by their value, on the one hand, and real chances for completion on the other: BATTLES LARGE ENOUGH TO MATTER, SMALL ENOUGH TO WIN.

The object is to break down overwhelming condemnations

into a number of small isolable items of potential action: to speak, if we must, of vast and sometimes circular causes of injustice and oppression, yet to encourage kids to go out anyway and open up a neighborhood day-care center, begin a picket line before the doorway of a racist banking corporation, organize a sit-down on the front steps of the landlord of a family of poor people in distress.

More clearly stated: The place to jam the gears of an unjust machine is where we stand, with quiet recognition of "the larger situation" in all cases, but with determination also to effect real changes *here and now* by means which are, in fact, within our range of dream and action.

I believe that we can spare our students a vast amount of needless grief by emphasizing an approach like this. The beginning of even the smallest move in the effort to undo a larger evil is the first step in a course of action that releases a person from self-accusation to begin the satisfying and rewarding struggle to make less the pain and the unfairness of the world.

It marks the difference between guilt and freedom.

11

It Is Evil to Tell Lies to Children

Many teachers, while irreverent in a number of other ways, appear to regard discussion of the flag pledge as too controversial for their taste. In justification of their own behavior, they often present an interesting but, I think, unpersuasive explanation. In the long run, they say, the content of the curriculum is not really so influential in the minds of children as are "the ways in which the student and the teacher can relate." For this reason, they believe, a matter as blunt and simple as the verbal content of a daily recitation need not be regarded as an issue of much import either way.

Very large numbers of entirely scrupulous teachers appear to share this point of view. It does not seem reasonable to speak of their position as if it were a conscious and disreputable evasion. It *is* an evasion, I believe, but not a conscious one, and it does rest upon a certain area of the truth. The process counts. There is no argument about this. Changes in the mode and manner of the classroom, without question, can democratize and humanize relationships. They do not, however, render possible a real subversion of the ideological bias that protects *this* class (this school, this neighborhood, these children) against a realistic recognition of the world of men and women in despair that stands on every side around them.

Few teachers would doubt that a democratized relationship among their students can be therapeutic and benign, but therapy will never be a substitute for social change. Teachers know very well that they will not undo the damage that is being done today within the U.S. schools if we can do no more than to prepare more wholesome, even-spirited and mutually respectful members of a sheltered, well-protected and anesthetic isolation chamber.

The flag pledge, being the most obvious form of pure indoctrination in the public school, is just exactly the variety of intellectual "content" that is now regarded with the most disdain by those who view the process of the school day as the sole point worth discussion. It is precisely for this reason, I believe, that it deserves the strong, intelligent and well-planned scrutiny and condemnation of those teachers who intend to change the public schools.

The longer we look at it, the more apparent it becomes that this is a peculiar—and a peculiarly undemocratic—exercise in several ways. First, it seems, more lucidly than any other lesson that we learn in public school, to leave exposed the true historic purpose of the institution. The time-honored objectives of the school and school board, in most other areas of education, are indirect, obscured by multiple contradictions, and at times benign in their appearance. Teachers and students cannot often look so openly upon the naked purpose of the school day.

Perhaps, therefore, we should be grateful for the flag pledge. Instead of futile protest or complaint, we ought to exploit the opportunity it presents. It tells our pupils, better than any other symbol, sign or lesson, both the name and nature of their landlord—or their keeper—for the years in which they are to be contained within the physical and psychological parameters of public school.

There are, I know, a large number of teachers who feel that they are compromised, and their intelligence insulted, by the obligation to enforce the recitation of this pledge. They struggle, however, to convince themselves and one another that the whole thing is a foolish unimportant custom with no power and no impact that endures. "We don't always do it anyway," some of these teachers say. Or else: "It doesn't work. We do it, but the kids don't really understand the words." The second statement has always seemed to me an odd excuse: If the kids don't even understand the words, why should a teacher ask them to recite it in the first place?

Veteran teachers know the truth of this only too well. The flag pledge "works." That symbol does not hang above the door for decoration. It is in the classroom for a very real and urgent purpose. A school or class that flies the flag makes an important declaration of intent. It makes it clear, no matter what we say we plan to do (and often really do intend) concerning free and open disputation in the course of public education, that there will be strict limits on all sides of our debate. Those limits are the limits of essential U.S. power and self-interest.

Certainly, many schools and many teachers do, at times, attempt to undercut the power of the recitation. There are also public schools where rituals like the pledge are very rapidly passed over—since the schools are eager to seem liberal and free. Even in these situations, nonetheless, most of us are well aware that exercises like the pledge do not cease to hold power. There is a familiar saying that the man who pays the piper calls the tune. The presence of the flag is our reminder of exactly who it is who pays the piper in our public schools. If we ever hope to have an open conversation, one that will not be contained with invisible restraints, it may well be that we will have to start either by taking down the flag or else by making clear, in vivid terms, the travesty and the self-contradiction which the flag pledge represents.

I do not believe that the recitation of the Pledge of Allegiance—or refusal to participate in such a ritual—has any connection with our loyalty as U.S. citizens. It does not have to do with either radical or conservative beliefs. It has to do with only one essential point: the plain and honest definition of the public school. If the school exists to serve the child and to guarantee the freedom of that child's mind, the flag should not remain.

Even beyond the bind on free discussion which the flag pledge represents, there is the troublesome matter that it simply is untrue as a description of the U.S.A. We do not live within "one nation indivisible." We live in at least two nations, skillfully and consciously divided by the genius of our real estate advisors and the red-line patterns laid out by the mortgage departments of our major banks. Again, liberty and justice, all too clearly, do not prove to be "for all." Instead, there is real liberty for a precious few—and the certitude of justice only for those who can retain the most experienced or prestigious lawyers.

Few of the teachers that I meet, at conferences and workshops, would bother to dispute these points. Many, however, try to handle the dilemma by attempting to "explain" the flag pledge to their pupils as a "dream" or "hope," and not an absolute description of the way things are. This tentative solution does not deal with the real problem. If the pledge is just a dream, an aspiration, then the wording ought to be revised. ("We pledge ourselves to find the ways to turn this segregated and divided nation into a just and decent land before we die.") Since this wording would be more obnoxious to the school boards than the alternative choice of just not saying it at all, it doesn't seem to help a teacher very much to offer this as a solution to the problem.

So far as I can see, there are two plausible options. One alternative is for a teacher to adhere to the decision handed down by the Supreme Court in the test case brought to Washington (and won) by the Jehovah's Witnesses in 1943, which denied the right of public schools to force a child to repeat the pledge.[21] (A later decision, on the part of a Federal Appeals Court in 1973, granted the same exemption to school-teachers.) Another alternative, adopted by some teachers, is to recite the pledge but then to invite the class to analyze the issue and, in cases of general agreement that the pledge is just plain fraudulent and incorrect, to aid and counsel the students to bring their protests to the public eye by urging them to present their arguments before the school board.

Whenever students do obtain a chance to pose their questions to the school board members, face to face, teachers ought to help them in advance to figure out the way to ask productive questions. Too many students, in situations of this kind, become uncharacteristically polite and tend to ask the people that they visit rather timid questions of the sort that politicians can expect. If our students suddenly grow shy and do this also, it is probable that they will get answers that we can anticipate. If it appears that this will be the case, we should at least encourage the class to plan ahead—to move beyond the first and obvious questions that they ask—in order to get to others that the school board cannot possibly predict.

Millions of students every year go off on a couple of "field trips" to the school board or the city hall. They tend to ask the same respectful questions as intimidated reporters at the White House. They end up with the same replies they could have read in their newspapers. There is a special skill in asking tough and searching questions—then in forcing answers which are not the old familiar kind that certain politicians almost always seem to have at hand.

As television viewers know quite well, it often takes an impolite reporter to obtain an interesting answer. I doubt that many kids can summon up sufficient nerve to ask aggressive and persistent questions to a school board of important (or of self-important) adults if we do not give them some explicit and quite pointed recommendations in advance.

Either of these suggestions seems to represent an avenue of logical dissent in the face of a dishonest obligation. The only form of personal reaction to the pledge which, to me, seems just plain unacceptable is to sit back and to do nothing in the way of protest. Sensitive teachers, finding themselves in similar situations, often say they feel uneasy but will add that they can see no possible alternative—unless they are prepared to lose their jobs.

Teachers who are genuinely troubled by this contradiction ought to recognize, from this point on, that there are many more viable options than they knew.

12

Code Expressions

I have postponed, perhaps too long, the most insidious and most bewildering of all forms of political indoctrination. These are the ever-present, repetitive and somewhat hypnotic forms of jingoistic propaganda that are conveyed by certain long-respected and seemingly immutable code expressions—words and phrases which clutter our texts, mislead our pupils and waste hours of our time in refutation.

Some of the most annoying instances of code expressions are, by this point in time, notorious. Many are the targets of considerable humor and sarcasm. In spite of their notoriety, however, they continue to prevail, uninterrupted, in the public schools. (Many things in public school are like this. It doesn't seem to matter how many books have proven them wrong or how many courts have judged them to be unconstitutional and illegal. Still they continue, like a grotesque and indestructible organism feeding on its own unloved position in the world around it.)

"Manifest destiny" is one of the most embarrassing of these phrases, being as it is a coverall for processes so brutal and, for several hundred years, entirely undisguised: the demolition of the life and culture of the North American Indians under the onslaught of a racist European population. Another phrase which has a similar effect and goal (either to disguise or to obscure a grave historic truth) is the "Good Neighbor Policy," a term which still lives on today—in face of all the evidence that any child or scholar could require—as the emblem of our national benefaction to the Latin countries.[22]

Of all such code expressions, perhaps the most transparent is the phrase "Free World." It is a peculiar phrase—one that pops up often in the textbooks, in the press and on TV. To many people, it might seem that the word *free* ought to have to do with something fair and honest: open to all possible points of view. It might mean, also, free food for people who are hungry and free doctors for the sick. It would be a stroke of great good luck for millions of poor people in those nations that we call the "Free World" if some little piece of this were true.

For many years, the term "Free World" has been used as a political code expression. It informs us of the presence of a nation that will fight beside our own, or side with us in diplomatic struggles, against the socialist nations of the world—or, as the texts label them, "the Soviet camp."

If a teacher were to sit down with a class and make a list of the nations now described within their textbooks as the "Free World," I suspect that there would be only a modest number (Great Britain, France and Canada, perhaps a dozen more) where the words might be at least half honest. There are many other lands, however, which are labeled "free" and yet are not free in any way that can be viewed with serious respect. The term "Free World" is one which must be adjusted every two or three years to include one or two new members and exclude three or four more. At the moment of this writing, the term includes all of the following: Argentina, Brazil, Haiti, Guatemala, Peru, the Dominican Republic, Chile, Uruguay, South Korea, South Africa, Pakistan and the Philippines. (Textbooks which were published prior to 1979 also include Nicaragua and Iran. These will doubtless be removed by the time of the next printing—and placed perhaps in the "uncertain" category.)

There are probably twenty or thirty other nations of this kind which public schools still designate as parts of the "Free World," but those listed above should be enough to demonstrate the actual function and intention of the code expression. Most of these governments hold in common certain basic traits: They kill, exile or imprison people who attempt to write "free" books or try to issue a "free" press. They channel large parts of their national resources into the pockets of the rich and leave the poor to starve or else to suffer lifelong malnutrition. Usually, they do not offer even token medical service to the poor. They make convenient military deals with the United States, giving us land to set up air force bases, harbors to provide both fuel and safety to our submarines and other naval craft and—in some cases—lend us mercenary soldiers if we should need them in what we have come to know as "brushfire" wars. They also make substantial business deals with U.S. corporations—companies like Polaroid, Gulf Oil, Xerox, General Motors, General Electric.

In plain terms, "Free World" ends up with three simple meanings: free opportunities for very large profits by the U.S. corporations; free use of land or harbors by the U.S. military; free opportunity for the uninhibited exploitation of the poor, carried out by the power of a self-serving upper class that operates in close collaboration with the military forces. These forces are often trained and almost always funded by the U.S. government.

If this is the case, why then do the textbooks still resort to such a devious code expression in discussion of these nations? Why do they use a phrase like "Free World" for a nation which is free in no regard—and does not wear even a mask of freedom? The answers to these questions are exactly the kinds of answers that lead students and teachers back into examination and re-examination of the reason for existence of the public school to start with.

The same scrutiny and the same objective (to raise essential issues of the function and the purpose of the public school) encourage many teachers also to examine certain other code expressions—"violent" and "peace-loving" are two—which the textbooks, press and politicians use with unabated fervor. Most of the textbooks state, with little hesitation, that the United States is a "peace-loving" nation. The president says it. The preachers repeat it. The majority of the population seems to feel at ease with the idea that this is really true. At the same time, it must be obvious to most adults that a very large part of our foreign policy depends entirely on the fact or threat of violent action to achieve our goals.

In recent years, teachers have sometimes been able to confront this very special set of loaded words by careful analysis and discussion with their pupils of the sale of arms by the United States to ninety-three foreign nations.[23] The sale of arms may not, in itself, be evidence of a nation's preference for a violent resolution of its problems. It is clearly evidence, however, that we do not find the handling of weapon sales distasteful or abhorrent.

Using the power of our weapons, governments in nations such as Guatemala, Chile and Brazil can kill off students who defend the poor, can exile, murder or imprison teachers who defend the students, and can murder innocent citizens who seek to stand up for their own rights and those of their teachers and professors. In view of our wistful tradition as a democratic nation which once fought a revolution of its own, teachers seem to me to be on firm and patriotic ground in asking students to address themselves to two specific, painful and uncomplicated questions: Why do we sell weapons to fascistic governments? Why do we sell weapons to a government that tortures its citizens and tramples on all shreds of human decency—in order to suppress all possibilities of democratic revolution?

If teachers succeed in pressing issues of this kind, leading to the point at which their students start to look into the profits that are made from sale of weapons to some of the most dehumanizing and oppressive nations in the world, it seems quite probable that many of those students will also begin to look with skepticism on the total spectrum of school-generated code expressions.

In situations of extreme distortion or self-contradiction on the part of text materials supplied to us by school officials, teachers do not need to stand up and declaim, denounce, exhort, before the children in the class. Instead, they only need to make available the facts and figures and, wherever possible (as always), to draw those figures from such reputable sources as UNESCO or the major TV networks or the established European and American press. With careful, detailed and responsible preparation, teachers can offer their pupils access to all data and documentation they could conceivably require in order to recognize the unjust and unshakable self-interest of the U.S. government in joining in commerce with those nations which we arbitrarily assign to the "Free World" in order to protect our economic power and our military strength.

It is self-evident that the moment at which a teacher begins to deal with issues quite so precious, quite so desperate and sacred to the mainstream of America, is also the moment at which that teacher, in all likelihood, arrives at the extreme and outer limits of all possible toleration on the part of even the most generous and progressive school officials. Whether or not the principal of the school should truly wish to extend protective power to a teacher in this situation, there is no way in which the teacher can expect that higher officials—members of the school board, for example—are going to accept such unconventional and, literally, subversive actions. Wherever else we might arrive at a point of no return, we surely will reach it once we have started to play havoc with those sanctified code expressions that defend the adult world from thinking.

It is at this point that politics and education come together in the most explicit, inextricable and provocative respect. This, then, will be the subject of the next two chapters.

13

Indoctrination vs. the Free Market of Ideas

Why must education be confused with politics at all?

Many teachers, even in the aftermath of all that they already know, still would like to tell themselves that education can be nonpolitical and neutral. It is not now. It has not been before. It will not be after we have finished with the struggles of our times. Teachers never can be neutral in the eyes of children. We are non-neutral by the clothes we wear. We are non-neutral by the kind of car we drive. We are non-neutral by the kinds of friends we choose, the books we read, the neighborhood in which we make our home. We are non-neutral, most of all, by the message of conviction or self-exile which is written in our eyes.

Since the teacher can't be neutral in the eyes of students, what then is the teacher's ethical answer to the propaganda sold to children in the textbooks which we are assigned to teach?

It may seem to many teachers that the choice is relatively simple: We either collude, connive, collaborate or else articulately rebel. (The foregoing, in any case, was once my own belief.) In my present view, however, none of this is so simple as it first appeared. Unless we designate the final word (*rebel*) in rather careful terms, I am afraid that we will end up in a dangerous position: one in which we effectively repeat the worst ingredients of that process of manipulation and control that we so passionately oppose. The ethical response to "bad indoctrination" is not something known as "good indoctrination." The sole response is: *no indoctrination.* The answer is a free and open market of ideas.

Schools, I have said, comprise the fourth largest business in the nation. It's notable, however—in a nation that professes to believe in the advantages of free and uninhibited competition in most areas of economic life—suddenly that principle disappears right at the classroom door. We've never been permitted to teach and learn within a free and competitive market of ideas. It is within the power of most teachers to *create* that kind of market; but, in order to do so, we will be obliged to go at least ten thousand light-years past the false and fragile options of the so-called "open classroom," "open corridor" or "open school."

In order to create a genuine free market, we have to find the courage to bring radical options into the consciousness of children—options which our supervisors, principals and school boards seldom have even dreamed about in years gone by and cannot be expected to approve.

The question, therefore, is how to go about it. Which options do we select? How do we choose them? How do we present them? With what intelligent and sensitive restraints? With what ambitious and compelling exaltation and imagination?

Many highly politicized teachers that I know are ready and willing to bring into their schools a viewpoint which is clearly ideological but, unhappily, in no respect conducive to real competition—one, to the contrary, which is angry, aggressive and intolerant in its unadulterated imposition of a radical point of view. Although I am convinced that I have often taught my classes in ways that do not differ greatly from the manner of unqualified imposition which these teachers recommend, I do not believe that it is an adequate or thoroughgoing answer to the problem that we face.

There are a number of reasons why I emphasize this point.

First, as always, there is a basic tactical consideration here as to the teacher's need for self-protection in the face of a predictable attack. Teachers who do not choose to spend another year in selling the ten significant ideas of Henry Kissinger to their class, but then replace them by the ten major beliefs of Mao Tse-tung, rapidly find themselves in an untenable situation. Those of their colleagues who do not share their views (and, very often, even those who do) will hurl at them the obvious charge of acting by unequal standards.

Once teachers have condemned the public schools for irresponsible indoctrination of the minds of children, those teachers end up in a dangerous position if they subsequently set out to sell to children their own exclusive body of beliefs instead— no matter how convinced they have become of the correctness of these views.

This is one of several reasons why I think that teachers make a serious mistake if they choose to use their classroom not just to confront the bias of the school, but to convert the students to their own political religion. Even in the wake of many hours of intelligent and well-meant "Disobedience Instruction," students will have no means by which to disobey *in interesting ways* if they know nothing but the gospel of the school and the rebellion of the teacher.

There is another reason why the teacher makes an unwise choice if he or she decides to stand up in the class and to confront the pupils with a set of doctrinaire slogans and rhetorical denunciations of the values represented by the school. Students by now have come to be anesthetized to counter-sloganeering. The words grow wearisome to the students before long. The teacher's views, having no prompt and vigorous counterfoil (the textbook hardly qualifies as such), cease to be catalytic in their provocations and become instead a tedious catalogue of shopworn phrases which, at best, may hypnotize but, more frequently, serve only to sedate.

There is a final reason why I do not think "indoctrination

from the Left" can be accepted as a viable answer to the bias now prevailing in the public schools. It is not a tactical matter, but a matter of fair play. For most students, as I have said, it doesn't seem to work particularly well. For a few, however, it works entirely too well—and unwisely. Students have the right to some sort of exemption from totalitarian control. Even if we should speak here only of one season, one semester or one year, still there is a dangerous lesson to be learned by children if the sole response to the indoctrination of the state is nothing better than indoctrination-in-reverse.

This is not to argue (after all that I have said already) that teachers should try to mute their own beliefs. It *is* to say that teachers must work very hard, and strive with all the ingenuity that they possess, first to steer away from propaganda, tyranny and unfair domination, second to build up a whole series of combative tactics in the consciousness of students long before we start to voice our own most forthright views, finally to provide those students with real substantive data, resources of every possible kind, in order to guarantee that their potential for revolt against our own rebellion will be serious—not token.

At this stage, we no longer are participating in a process of indoctrination-in-reverse—but rather in an ongoing exercise of intellectual energies in vigorous cross fire. In order to create an atmosphere so vital and so strong, teachers need to make available a very broad spectrum of contradictory ideas, materials and leads to outside forms of information.

Teaching in this kind of classroom takes a lot more work than do traditional methods of instruction, but the rewards are greater—sometimes spectacular—and, so far as I can see, there is no other ethical option for a serious teacher in a time of torment and in an unjust and bewildered land.

Postscript: Insisting on the Real Thing

Once we determine, by whatever means, to create the sense of option that allows our students to dissent with us in competent and effective ways, we then must do the work it takes to build a situation where the choices are not superficial. The contrast here is between two wholly different terms: authentic "choice" and inauthentic "whim."

Even the most progressive and enlightened of our public schools opt for the second almost every time. Following the lead of the romantic school reformers of the 1960s, they argue that the vigorous and provocative information which a sensitive and irreverent child may require will come to the child through "natural processes" of totally spontaneous and organic generation. This point of view is innocent but naïve.

Significant political data of the kind that genuinely counts never spontaneously occurs to students in the public schools unless somebody takes some pains to let them know that it is "there." It is like the situation in an airport lounge. No one, of his own free will, is going to buy a ticket to fly to Rio de Janeiro if he does not first know it exists.

In most of the so-called "open" schools that flourished in the early 1970s, many of which still carry on today, children have their choice between a lot of nonpolitical and harmless options: gerbil cages, batteries and bulbs, balance scales and other gadget-oriented learning tools. In political and literary terms, the students in these classrooms have a similarly circumscribed frame of ethical decision. They "freely chose" between the latest "issue booklets," published by a branch of Xerox Corporation, little plug-in film-and-listening centers shipped into the school by I.B.M., or programmed reading kits produced by S.R.A. (a corporate affiliate of I.B.M.), and then, for conflict, search through photo-booklets produced by Time Incorporated or else by Little, Brown (a publishing company wholly owned by Time). For radical contrast, they can get the latest news out of *My Weekly Reader* (also owned by Xerox).

The point is not that school materials need to represent a full array of every possible point along the spectrum of political beliefs, but they must represent a *significant* array—or else we might as well give up the effort altogether.

One of the best ways to determine whether students have

been given an authentic set of choices, I suggest, is by demanding a response to one specific question: "Is there anything here within this room to keep a child wide awake at night with painful self-examination? Is there anything here which can compel the students to confront, not just the textbooks and not just their teacher, but *themselves* as well with questions that might warrant a legitimate debate?"

My own personal choice of classroom options runs the full range from political data on the struggles of poor people in Brazil and Chile, Paraguay, Guatemala, Haiti and Peru, to the intelligent (but, in my own view, inaccurate) refutations available in such right-wing publications as *The National Review* and *Business Week*. If there is not at least this limited degree of confrontation present and available to pupils, then I do not see how we can honestly pretend that students have had access to conflicting attitudes and information on a level that commands their serious respect.

Teachers do not need to go to the absurd degree of trying to bring all *possible* viewpoints into play within their public schools. Nor do teachers need to make an effort to pretend that all ideas are "equally correct" or "equally worthwhile." Quite to the contrary, my point of view insists that they are *not*. Teachers, instead, are asked to do their best to argue for the primacy of their own views within a free, yet fervent, field of competition.

I naturally assume that teachers with political positions very different from my own (including those of extreme conservative belief) will wish to enter the competition I propose. There is no way to avoid this competition, and I do not see why we should wish to do so. It would be a more exciting nation—and, I am convinced, a more enlightened one—if students were given the chance to grapple with a multiplicity of ideologies and points of view.

No one can possibly argue for a particular point of view as well as the man or woman who believes it. Those to the left of political center in this country often react with considerable alarm to this idea: especially if it means that people such as William Buckley were to be given the chance not just to "be heard" within our public schools, but rather to *persuade,* to *argue,* to *win over.* ("What kind of an education would it be if someone such as William Buckley were allowed to win the ears of high school students in the morning—and someone such as I. F. Stone or Dr. Spock during the afternoon?" My own reaction is to view this prospect with incredible excitement. At long last we might begin to teach our children how to think.)

As for the sense of danger that so many liberal-leftists seem to feel, I do not understand the reason for their fear. I have no doubt but that my own ideas will ultimately win out within the minds of children. But this is because I really do believe my viewpoints are correct and that truth has a power of its own. It is my own suspicion that a great many liberals really don't believe this. It is for this reason that they often settle for the boring kingdom of consensus, rather than to place their views in opposition to articulate adversaries. Like many conservatives, it seems that what they fear the most is not the potential power of another person's point of view, but rather the extreme fragility of their own. But that is just another excellent reason why we need to change the schools.

If, in the first six grades of school, the teacher's continuous contact with the class creates a situation that appears to make all dissident viewpoints seem ridiculous or unacceptable, not only due to the personal power of an individual teacher but also, and more likely, due to the affection which the children in the room will feel for their own teacher, then I suggest once more that other teachers in the school—or else community people—who definitely *do* dissent be given the chance to join the class, not once or twice, but on a routine basis.

It seems important to conclude this chapter by restatement of a dual point that I have made before. Indoctrination, in order to work, must be totalitarian; it must take place within a vacuum. We seek, instead, to achieve a high degree of moral and political democracy within the class. Teachers, as I have said, do not need to offer every point of view with equal force. Most of us—we might as well be frank—will offer our own as powerfully as we can, because we know that our pupils will be ready to fight back, that we have provided the weapons to fight back, and that there are other teachers who will fight back also. So there *is* bias. There *is* persuasion. It is not, however, indoctrination-in-reverse.)

Teachers have the right to say what they believe without the fear of accusation or self-accusation. No student, however, should be forced to suffer social ostracism, nor compelled to pay a price, beyond that of the moral anguish of the issue in itself, for taking a stance in opposition to that of the teacher. Both conditions can, and must, be realized by an ethical teacher in rebellion against all that is implied, inflicted or reflected by the standard dogmatism of the textbooks, the curricula and the time-embedded customs and conventions that prevail today within the U.S. public schools.

14

Patriots with Blinders

The argument is raised, in opposition to almost every sentence that has been written in this book, that every social order needs a certain amount of political indoctrination in order to maintain its own cohesive character. It is argued that, particularly in the context of the 1980s, with ominous signs of class and ethnic conflict that might splinter the nation in a dozen different ways, the last thing we can possibly afford is a disintegration of the uniform traditions represented by the standard textbooks and conventional schoolteachers.

Even those teachers who do not share this belief, and who do not see social disintegration as the danger which so many citizens perceive, must nonetheless be prepared to deal with this concern. Not everybody who will raise this issue is necessarily reactionary in political position. Some are alarmed that uncontrollable turmoil will result from presentation to young people of that spectrum of divergent and conflicting views that I propose. For all of these reasons, we must be ready to defend our own position with a number of reflective answers.

First of all, in trying to deal with opposition or anxiety concerning dangers of disintegration, the point can be made that school indoctrination of the kind we face today does not succeed, in ultimate terms, in reaching patriotic goals. The short-term victory is indisputable: little students standing to salute the U.S. flag, bigger students—sometimes only ten years older—marching to war beneath that flag, and singing patriotic songs. The long-term goal, however, is lost repeatedly, because we seldom do succeed in educating either rational or long-lasting patriots. The archaic methods that we use will not survive the test of either truth or time, except in the cases of those who have agreed to cordon off all access to new information and ideas that might enable them to grow in understanding as historical conditions change.

To those who are troubled by the possible risk of chaos and conformity in failing to forge a uniform consciousness of patriotic loyalty among our boys and girls, teachers can make the point that what we now produce—in terms of patriots or citizens—is something totally different from the sensible and democratic goals of those who helped to found the nation. Either we turn out mindless and unthinking soldiers for our predatory or (as we like to say) mistaken wars, or else we turn out numb and acquiescent people who experience, at most, a vague malaise about the actions of the rest but end up doing little more than to sit back before the TV screen and offer impotent remarks about it all. There is another frequent outcome, too. This is the situation of the man or woman who has been protected from the truth for twelve long years (or sixteen years, if he or she has been through college also), then goes to pieces at the first exposure to the fact that we, like almost every other major nation, do a vast amount of evil on this earth. A narrow-minded and protected patriotic dogmatism is both perilous and frail.

Shall we produce fake patriots with blinders—protected by well-fabricated lies—or honest patriots, prepared to live with knowledge of both good and evil in our land, restless to root out the second, passionate to reinforce the first?

This is a question that has at least a chance of winning listeners to our point of view. It is a blunt appeal to the self-interest of sophisticated and farsighted parents. If they love their children, they may be willing to think hard about the dangers of a sheltered nationalism and false patriotic pride that shatters at first contact with the truth.

The goal, as it is designated here, is not to undermine and to subvert ("deschool") society, but only to open up the windows and let in fresh air—along with a free market of ideas. If the traditional values of the nation can survive in contestation of this kind, then they will thrive and grow far more emphatic by the competition. If they cannot, then possibly they do not merit the devotion of our students in the first place.

Three hundred years ago, John Milton wrote these words: "Let [Truth] and Falsehood grapple. Who ever knew Truth put to the worse in a free and open encounter?"[24] If the more conservative parents of our school and neighborhood are alarmed at the idea of that encounter, there is a relevant question to be asked: How much can a citizen believe in those ideas which represent the heart and soul of an American tradition if he or she does not even dare to see those values stand the test of conflict from outside?

It is probably true that there can never be a totally free and open contest of ideas. It is quite possible, nonetheless—with a good, exciting mix of teachers from one level to the next—for an imaginative school to come extremely close. Most public schools do not even try to offer the free and open contest I propose. It is in the power of our teachers, nonetheless, not just to build that cross fire in the classroom, but to defend it on entirely reasonable grounds.

Those who treasure blind obedience, in their nation, in their children or in their own immediate subordinates in life, will doubtless continue to wonder whether an open competition of this kind will tend to undermine the selfish interests of the U.S. corporations or the U.S. government itself during the years to come. It seems to me these people ought to think a little more about the ways in which a nation does, or does not, win allegiance in the world beyond its own frontiers. There has been much talk in the United States of wishing to win the hearts and minds of people in the Third World. It ought to be apparent by this time that we will never win the hearts and minds of people who are victims of our corporate predation with bigger bombs and more expensive gifts of automatic rifles and jet planes. There is, however, at least an outside chance that we may win some badly needed friends if we can educate a generation of young people with an ethical sensitivity to the needs and aspirations of all human beings, whether they live in Boston, San Francisco or Bombay.

The breadth of compassion that can be implanted in our students during the early years of school ought to be valued for its own sake. But the same quality, the same compassion and the same capacity to open our minds to viewpoints, ideologies and longings that are different from our own, may also be viewed as the highest form of intelligent self-interest. The starving masses of the earth, who still must struggle daily for the bare necessities of life—for food, clean water, health care, housing, labor, literacy and the like—will choose their political allies and potential friends, at least in part, on the basis of the active ethics which those friends and allies seem to represent. Military strength and the calculating use of our capacity for economic benefaction seem to be losing value in the geopolitical world that is developing today. Small-minded citizens who cannot see beyond the dollar margin in our international relations or cannot conceive of foreign trade agreements other than those that bring us immediate military opportunities or possible inroads into profitable markets are no longer working in the long-term interests of our country as a whole.

If certain groups, leaders and entire populations in the Third World speak at times with admiration for the people and the symbolism of this nation, it is because of the spoken words, the writings and traditions represented by our poets and our prophets—not our dollars, not our color TV consoles, not our jet planes and our guns. This, then, is a selfish argument for the education of unselfish people. It is the best way we can arm ourselves for a world in which war will, before long, have been outdated by the longing for survival and efficacious human love.

American foreign policy, for several generations, has been solidly resting on a narrow definition of our military, economic and political self-interest. One of the direct results of this behavior is our willingness to export military weapons, or to grant funds for military aid, to nations which, by all humanitarian standards, have no claim upon our friendship or allegiance. We deal with these nations solely on a basis of cold-blooded, short-term and immediate self-interest.

The most conspicuous example of short-term interest is our sale of weapons to South Africa. In this situation, we have not only sold weapons to one of the outstanding racist governments on earth but have done so in the face of worldwide protest.

On August 7, 1963, then later the same year (December 4), the United Nations issued a request, known as a "solemn call," asking member nations not to sell more weapons to South Africa. The American government, however, did not choose to alienate a useful ally. Nor did we intend to let our corporations lose a favored trading partner. It was our decision, therefore, to defy the plea of the U.N. From 1962 to 1968, according to the Department of Defense, U.S. companies sold military goods worth twenty-five million dollars to South Africa. In 1969, according to the Pentagon, South Africa was the second largest customer for U.S. weapons on the continent of Africa. One of the attractions was the fact that South Africa could pay us for our guns in gold. Another was this: Sixteen percent of all uranium, at that time, came from South Africa.[25]

The U.S. government defended its sale of weapons to South Africa on the grounds that the U.N. did not forbid the sale of weapons. It issued only a solemn plea. Today our government would probably maintain that we no longer sell our military hardware to South Africa. Whether or not this is the case we have no way to know, since the C.I.A. has asserted in public its continued intention to do whatever it must in service of our national self-interest. Even if the present prohibition should be absolute, however, it is too late to make up for the damage we have done. Unlike the unsafe automobiles which seem to have become one of our major items of domestic sale, attack planes, automatic rifles and rocket launchers cannot be "re-called."

The weapons we sold to South Africa throughout the period of a decade past are used today as instruments of repression in the struggle of white rulers to contain insurgent blacks. Teachers might find it of interest to read to their pupils certain of the news-dispatches on this subject from various papers such as *The New York Times*. How can a school board fire a teacher for reading an article from a paper like *The Times*?

Those same weapons were also used in 1978 when the South African government chose to invade the newly independent nation of Angola. It was South Africa's heavily armed invasion of Angola which offered the Cuban government either a moral or, in any event, politically convincing pretext to send in tens of thousands of troops to help to defend Angola against a well-armed, white and racist government.

At a point in time when American policy toward African liberation had begun to undergo some modest reconsiderations, we found ourselves—whether we liked it or not—the objects of considerable contempt among the leaders of black Africa. Their enemy, after all, was armed with weapons manufactured in Ohio, Oregon, Texas and Connecticut—"made in the U.S.A." We found ourselves aligned in the eyes of the Third World with one of the two or three most hated governments in recent history. The Cubans today are demonized in the U.S. press, while the U.S. government is demonized throughout black Africa. Who can have gained from these series of transactions—except for the owners of certain U.S. corporations and the brutal and white-dominated government of South Africa?

Postscript

Many Americans, and too many of our students, have not yet had an opportunity to stop and understand how fast the world is changing. Sooner or later, teachers themselves have got to make up for the time lag represented by the textbooks and TV.

American citizens can afford no longer to place their conscience second and a patriotic banner first. Teachers cannot afford to yield to pressure from the school boards or the P.T.A. to place the lives of U.S. citizens above the lives of at least four billion other human beings. It is, in any case, a meaningless division. In the present age, national flags and patriotic slogans will not offer anyone protection from the nightmare of a nuclear war. Super-American patriots with blinders—and billions of men and women in all nations with their eyes wide open and uplifted to the sun—will die together in the holocaust of nuclear disaster.

The Pledge of Allegiance becomes a recitation of psychosis, the "Star Spangled Banner" becomes an anthem for the mad, in the wake of Hiroshima and the evolution of the hydrogen and neutron bombs. We were not hired to train our pupils for insanity.

This, then, is one additional reason for the argument I make within this chapter. There is the argument for honest and responsible patriots. There is the argument against the danger of false patriots who fall apart at their first glimpse of the real world. There is the argument for winning some small bits of loyalty or friendship on this earth, not because we can afford to *buy* it but because our national character might *deserve* it. With all of the rest, there is the question of survival. Surely there is ample ammunition here for any teachers who should speak out of their hearts and then discover that they must be ready to defend themselves, in face of community critics or their academic peers.

It is one of those ultimate issues about which a conscientious teacher simply has no choice.

15

A Time When Certain Things Are Not Allowed

There is a dangerous fashion gathering followers in the United States today. It began six or seven years ago, but it is only coming into its maturity today. It goes somewhat like this.

Social protest and active struggle against the kinds of societal injustice which are described throughout this book are permissible only under certain conditions, at certain stated periods of time and, above all, only in the decade (era, period) specifically assigned to social activism by the press and by TV.

The 1960s represented one of those periods in which protest and visible action on the various aspects of our protest were okay. They were okay because there were certain prominent black leaders at the helm. They were okay because the manifestations of struggle provided a fascinating light show for TV and an ongoing narrative for newspapers and magazines. They were okay especially (and this is the most insidious of all) because "people did such things at that time"—*at that time, in those years, in that decade, but not now.*

Sometimes, when I write or speak on a subject that troubles me and for which I am hoping to suggest a possible solution, somebody will observe in a critical review or essay: "It is amazing. He really sounds as if he thinks that he is living still in 1965."

I do not think that we are still living in 1965.

I think that we are living in the 1980s.

I refuse to accept the myth that somebody in a skyscraper penthouse in New York City, or in a newspaper office anywhere else in the United States, can abrogate the power to designate appropriate hours or decades for the moral or amoral purposes which *they* believe to be acceptable.

We write about social change—or, in this instance, about a plan to gather our forces to transform the public schools—not by asking permission from those people who presently live well (or perhaps not even well at all) in the wire mesh of economic avarice and despair which they have decreed to be the only proper moral texture for the 1980s.

We write, protest, struggle and make changes whenever we are moved, compelled or feel the personal energy to do so. Many teachers feel as I do on this subject and they do not intend to allow their actions to be orchestrated by those people who sell tennis gear, nostalgic movies, jogging shoes—or justice.

Editors will, I suppose, go right on attempting to control and manipulate each decade. If they must, they will also continue, in their innocence or cruelty, to assign each year to its appropriate activities: lethargy to one year, justice to the next year, roller-skating (greed or narcissism) to the next.

We have never consented to protest on assignment. We will speak of these matters—of each struggle, of each mandate, of each passion—when we must.

PART II

Grass Roots
Organizing Parents
and Teachers
for Collective Strength

1

Building a Base of Trust and Friendship with the Parents

Nothing is possible unless we organize.

Teachers need to organize not just among themselves, but also with the parents of their students—and, in all possible cases, with the students too. This is the case, at least, if they have any hope to win the loyalty of friends for times of confrontation that will frequently result from almost any acts of conscience they may choose to undertake in order to transform the public schools.

The organizing sequence I am going to describe begins with parents, proceeds to fellow teachers and ends up in consideration of the ways that we can build a sense of mutual protection with the students in our schools.

In seeking support among the parents of the neighborhood and school, a teacher's initial actions ought to be informal and relaxed. The first goal is not to build a political structure, but rather to establish a sense of private loyalty and personal affection with even a limited number of parents and community leaders in the neighborhood nearby.

One of the most natural ways to go about this is to establish a regular habit of late-afternoon or early-evening visits to a student's home, ideally under circumstances which will not be sterilized and frozen by that atmosphere of falsified friendliness that undermines so may parent-teacher consultations. This is not, at first sight, either a radical or original prescription—nor does it appear particularly subversive. The truth, however, is that visits and informal relationships like these are seldom possible if we observe the orders of our principals or the dictates of our teacher education.

Teachers have been taught for generations to avoid such vulnerable liaisons with the parents of the children whom they teach. As a result, most of us have forever been restricted to the classic situation of the parent-teacher conference in the corner of our room at 2:15, after the class has been dismissed and nervous parents timidly appear. Neither the parents nor the teachers seem to like these meetings very much. The same is true of those mechanical home visits that some of the more progressive principals will now and then allow. The purpose and the situation are both awkward and unreal.

Few teachers feel at ease in making these professional visits: antiseptic sessions set up in advance in order to discuss the student's academic progress, peer relationships or learning difficulties. Most effective teachers who have built up good relations with the parents of their class tell me that they try to make a point to visit parents only under sociable conditions which can overcome these needless inhibitions.

The purposes of the type of visit I propose are totally different from those that lie behind conventional home visits. The goal, indeed, is not professional at all. Instead it is to begin to know our students and their folks not as our "clients," but as our allies and our friends. The best way that I know to bring about this goal is to time our visits to a student's home in such a way as to accord with certain normal social rituals—like dinner. Mothers and fathers seem to find it natural to chat, to offer us a beer or a glass of wine, and now and then will ask: "Have you had supper?"

If we have not, very few parents that I know will let us leave until we do.

If I had not spoken with so many teachers in the past few years, I would not feel so free to generalize from my own re-

warding memory of many evenings of this kind. Other teachers speak to me repeatedly, however, of the same response. It
is not long before the parents and the teachers begin to feel a
sense of common cause.

This is, by intention, a modest way to start. It is only naive
organizers, in my point of view, who think that they can jump
right into massive organizing schemes, rally the neighborhood
and pack the hall, without a long internship (as I think it properly might be called) in building up of natural loyalties, warm
feelings of affection each for each, between at least some of
the parents and at least some portion of the teachers in the
school.

Parents who might deeply disagree with some of our professional or political ideals often find themselves our friends and
allies long before they have a chance to think about our ideologies or pedagogic views. By this stage, they are likely to
support us, if support is needed, on the grounds of plain affection and fair play. One week in the last part of September, we
are having supper and discussing the World Series. Six
months later, friendships made across that dinner table have
been turned into a political allegiance in the sort of confrontation that explodes, at times we least expect, into the public
eye.

I know a small number of principals who actually encourage
their teachers to build up these easy and informal friendships;
but these men and women are unusual. Most principals do not
approve of social get-togethers of this kind. As a young
teacher, I was seriously reprimanded by my principal for stop-
ping in each morning before class to buy myself a little cream-
filled cupcake, called a "Twinkie," at the corner grocery. She
told me that informal access on the part of neighborhood people would diminish my position as a "school professional."

The reasons for administrative opposition to these natural
forms of parent-teacher contact are diverse. Sometimes they
are innocent and well intended. The principal wants to protect

us from imagined dangers. More often, the reasons are devious and self-serving. Many principals seem to live in constant terror that the direct friendships which evolve from normal behavior of this kind will undermine their power over parents (a power that depends upon the parents' lack of detailed information in regard to the real status of their kids) and over the teachers (power which is based on an implanted fear of an unknown community). As a result, a principal will often take considerable pains to frighten teachers with the dangers of informal social contacts: "Don't go out of your way to visit with the parents. Let the parents come to *you*. If you are obliged to visit for some reason, then at least be certain that you don't lose sight of your professional behavior."

The term *professional,* by this rigid definition, comes very close to meaning a false smile and a frozen jaw: a kind of Maginot Line of artifice and ice. The same principal who warned me of the dangers of a visit to the corner store carried her warnings even to the point of detailed dinner-table admonitions: "If you are asked if you would like a drink, try to say no. If there isn't any way to turn it down without offense, then at least be sure to limit it to one—and drink it very, very slowly."

Talk of this nature strikes some people as amusing. It is tragic, however, that attitudes like these are so familiar and pervasive. The principal's concern, as stated, is for the loss of our "professional" protection in the face of an imagined danger—and, in part, of course, this may well be the truth. The deeper motive is, too frequently, the principal's alarm concerning the extent of his or her unquestioned power to give orders, to manipulate and to control.

If certain principals could have it as they like, parents would never have a chance to meet the teacher other than by mediation of the school administration in itself. In such a way, administrators constantly restabilize their power. Once the parents get to know the teacher on their own, there is no longer any way for school officials to restrict parental access to unseemly data on the reading levels, cumulative records and the other inner workings of a public school. Nor is there any means by which to limit teacher access to the loyalty of parents in the case of later difficulties with the school system itself.

All the worst fears of the school administration prove time and again to be quite justified. Parents do begin to trust those teachers who join them, first for social reasons only, later to divulge some of those areas of previously forbidden data which would otherwise remain beyond their reach. Teachers, on the other hand, begin to understand that in the case of a real showdown later on they will have a lot of good friends right in the neighborhood to stand up at their side.

The sense of intimacy increases even more once teachers start to join in far more carefully organized meetings with the parents of their pupils in a local church or other meeting place. The stakes are raised again, and friendships with the parents grow more natural and deep, once teachers start to join in neighborhood projects—a weekend's renovation of an empty lot, for instance, technical aid in setting up a tenant's union or—if the need should lend itself to such behavior—in the presentation of a set of neighborhood demands to members of the city council or the mayor.

Teachers who are working in suburban schools sometimes observe that there are very few clear-cut opportunities to demonstrate a personal loyalty of this kind: not, at least, in a manner so explicit as would be the case within an urban ghetto or a rural slum. The issues that concern suburban neighborhoods tend to be less urgent and overt.

In every neighborhood, nonetheless, teachers discover, sooner or later, certain issues of immediate importance to the parents of their pupils. Most of these issues have to do with problems in the schools themselves. Here, too, teachers frequently observe that it inevitably helps to reinforce their own position if they are prepared to do some work to help to advance those issues that are most important to the people in the neighborhood.

In such a way, the teacher has a chance to be an equal and active member of the school community. In ceasing to be a professional artifact, the teacher does not become a condescending moralist nor an intrusive agitator, but simply an ally, a co-worker and a friend.

2

Beyond Friendship:
Teaching Basic Skills

The previous chapter speaks of winning friendship. This one
speaks of ways to win respect.

No matter how much we may speak of larger issues; no
matter how much we may wish to speak of racist patterns,
policies, curricula, in talking to the parents in an inner-city
school, parents need, above all else, to ascertain that we will
listen carefully to *their* concerns—concerns which often have
to do with nothing more elaborate or more lofty, at the start,
than issues of the basic mental health of their own children,
or the sane, sequential and effective teaching of essential
skills. All the rent strikes, neighborhood meetings, nights of
fun and friendship and the rest count for nothing if the parents live with an unspoken anguish about reading, writing,
math and other bread-and-butter matters of this kind.

Teachers, however, who intend to offer reassurances to parents have got to be prepared to come across with the real
goods. The "real goods"—reading, writing, math—are not so
easy for all teachers to deliver. Many young teachers, indeed,
are not at all convinced that matters so tedious and ordinary
as "the basic skills" are nearly so important as the parents of
their children ardently believe.

It is hard to say this and not seem to turn against some of
my former friends. Nonetheless, I think that teachers who intend to win the loyalty of students, yet wish to do so at the

least expenditure of their own energy and time, often make the serious mistake of thinking that a minimum of hard work and a maximum of whimsical diversion will prove the perfect formula for student adulation.

The quickest way to forfeit parent backing, even if it wins some short-term ego satisfaction in the friendliness of pupils, is to sail off on a Summerhillian journey of ecstatic and spontaneous adventures, at cost of all substantial day-to-day hard labor in the areas of basic skills.

It has become a commonplace, among too many idealistic converts to the cause of school reform, to speak of themselves as if they were not teachers any longer, but some sort of "incidental person" who just happens to be present among children in the school. Apart from the fact that sensible parents will react with great uneasiness in the face of meandering resource persons with this aimless point of view, there is also the fact that educational abdication of this kind rapidly drives the class into exhaustion—and the nation as a whole into a state of mind which now begins to rally under the banner: "BACK TO BASICS."

This kind of behavior, on the teacher's part, bores the pupils, denies the teacher's genuine superiority of accumulated knowledge and ruins any chance of realistic solidarity between a conscientious teacher, sensible students and responsible parents. In place of innovation, we end up with collective tedium, communal apathy, an innovative void.

In the course of a recent visit to an English class in "Modern Fiction" at a relatively innovative and expensive prep school in New England, I asked the students a casual question about the work that was in process that semester: "What novels have you read?"

There was a pause before one student told me that they hadn't yet "got into books" because they hadn't yet made up their minds on how they ought to settle on the prior issue of "which books to read" and "who should make the choice." If this process had consumed only two weeks, perhaps the student's voice would not have carried quite so much despair. Two months had passed, however, and they still were locked up in that hopeless trap of trying to decide how to proceed and by what rules they and their teacher ought to "settle" on which books they ought to read—and in what order!

One student, a bright and articulate young man, spoke up at last: "You know what I wish? I wish that on the first day of the term our teacher had come in, slammed down a book by William Faulkner on the table, told us that he thought it was a good book and asked us to take it home and read it in a week. If we didn't like it, then we could have come back in and told him so. Maybe we would have got fed up with Faulkner and gone off instead to find some other American writers—maybe Hemingway or F. Scott Fitzgerald. Or else we might have liked the book a lot and gone right on and read a dozen more by the same man. Either way, there would have been some food out on the table. At least we wouldn't have had to spend two months discussing how we felt about an empty plate."

This incident occurred in a twelfth-grade class. The same issues inevitably prevail for teachers at all levels. Whether within a rich suburban village or in the poorest urban slum, students grow weary, parents grow alarmed, if they begin to feel that we, as teachers, are benign and well intending, but that nothing serious is really going on.

In certain suburban situations, where pupils have already had some good skill training in the first six years of school, teachers of the kind I have described may find that there will be a longer interval of time before the parents start to demonstrate alarm. In a poor neighborhood, by contrast, teachers will be granted very little chance to make their case (or, simply to make friends) if they cannot first manage to put something that resembles "bread and butter"—reading, math and writing—on the tables of those arid and despairing schools.

Some responsibility for these recent inhibitions, on the part of decent but intimidated teachers, has to be placed upon the doorstep of romantic authors who have led such teachers to believe that there is no third option between old-time tyranny and innovative abdication. If this were so, if there were not something very important and very much worthwhile in between, we might as well give up the game right now.

Many beginning teachers who have had an overdose of those euphoric but unrealistic writings of the early 1970s— what has been designated as "the literature of pedagogic laissez faire"—often make a serious mistake in failing to respect the real concern of many parents that their children may no longer have the means to manage and to cope within a technologically complex society. If a teacher can possibly convey to parents from the start that he or she is solid, sober and prepared to live with the realistic incubus of being an adult (hence, knowing more than children about certain things and being prepared to share what we *do* know without infuriating rituals of indirection), from that point on we can begin to win the loyalty of very large numbers of the parents of our pupils— and we can do so in a relatively short time.

Certain teachers will argue and debate forever as to whether or not they ought to bother to teach reading—all of this because they are convinced that any pupil who "really wants to read" will somehow lose himself in *Moby Dick* or *War and Peace* "at the right moment"—and just "read it on his own." Talk of this sort strikes me as a colossal fraud. It happens like that maybe once out of a thousand times. Moreover, it is not difficult to teach a child to read: to do so, furthermore, by any one of the many diverse and nonmanipulative methods, several of which are listed in the last part of this book.

In view of these facts, a teacher who seeks the loyalty and future back-up of a community of parents ought to refuse to let the issue of hard skills grow into a serious divisive force between himself (herself) and those whom he (or she) intends to win as allies for the years ahead. If this recommendation were to mean the sacrifice of every principle and every dream within a teacher's heart and soul—if, in addition, it appeared that teaching kids to read would be a long, unending process that would take up the entire day, entire month, entire year— then there might be reason to debate this matter as a central issue for defiance or capitulation.

It *doesn't* take up the entire day, entire month, entire year, however, and it need not represent capitulation to all other goals and principles a teacher might hold dear. For this reason the easiest thing, it seems to me, is to get into it, get on with it and show some measurable progress in the course of several weeks.

It isn't long before the consequences of a teacher's work in basic skills become quite obvious to those outside the school. Parents start to pick up rapidly on news like this. Many have no idea at all of what the teacher's politics might be. It doesn't seem to matter much to anyone concerned, so long as certain *other* things seem to be right. Then, too, with rare exceptions, the school administration—faced with something which it cannot help but recognize as effective progress—tends to leave the class and teacher relatively alone. All the principal cares, for now, is that the room is quiet, the kids are working, they appear to be learning, and the parents aren't complaining anymore.

There surely are thousands of ways of going about the task of organizing parents. One of the most obvious of all must be apparent to the reader by this time: If the teacher teaches, and if the students learn, and if the parents and the principal begin to sense some genuine peace and continuity within the class from day to day, a plenitude of shocking statements or political provocations on the teacher's part seem to be forgivable or, at worst, beside the point. Getting something done that can be seen, tested or tasted—reading and writing—words and num- bers coming to life, like so many jumping beans, within a child's mind—this, for sure, so far as teachers are concerned, is one of the very best starting points for any subsequent organizing goals.

Up to this point I've raised the issue of hard skills solely as a tactic, or a precondition, for the building of alliances with the parents of the pupils in our class. There is at least one other serious reason to argue for effective reading, writing and math skills among those boys and girls who we may hope to grow someday into the ethical rebels of a generation yet to come. This is the simple point of basic power, competence, survival in the student's navigation of a complicated and increasingly perplexing world. If, as teachers, we would like to think that we can take an active role in seeking to render less intense the pain, injustice, disproportion in the world, we cannot sensibly agree to educate our students to be the beautiful, bold, but useless warriors of social change.

The need is for a generation of hard-working, ethically motivated and effective rebels: people who do not choose to leave the skills of numbers and of scientific competence to the engineers of Westinghouse and I.B.M., who do not choose to leave the competence of words and word persuasion to the managers, scriptwriters and producers of the major television networks. If those young men and women who now are students in the public schools intend someday to write a powerful press release in order to argue for a moral cause which they uphold, I see no reason why it should be one bit less effective than those statements which their corporate adversaries will be writing in return.

Why should we leave the skills of basic competition and survival to the people in the banks, the big insurance companies and corporations, or else to those within the Pentagon and C.I.A.? We cannot afford to leave the skills of numbers to the corporations that control us, the skills of reading to the advertising corporations that deceive us, the skills of writing to those governmental agencies that issue orders to young people which they scarcely comprehend but do not dare to disobey.

This is just one of many reasons why responible teachers should no longer feel inhibited, or reluctant, to attempt, with all their energy and imagination, to deliver hard, combative and effective skills to those who may, before long, choose to carry on the struggles we have only managed to begin.

3

Building Loyalties
Among the Teachers

In the last two chapters I have spoken chiefly about building
up liaisons with the parents of the students in our schools.
This chapter and the next one will address the various ways of
building loyalties among the teachers and the kids.

Any grass-roots organizing process among teachers ought to
be distinguished, at the start, from organizing efforts that take
place inside one or the other of the major unions. This does
not mean that we should turn our backs on powerful and immensely influential organizations of this kind. I think that
those who *can* should work, wherever possible, through vehi-
cles like these but not as docile cogs within one or another of
two vast and intricate machines. The role appropriate to those
of rebel and irreverent disposition—who nonetheless decide to
take their stand within the N.E.A. or A.F.T.—ought to be that
of intelligent critics, companionable gadflies, a quiet conscience working always from within.

As a classroom teacher, I was a member of the N.E.A. for
several years and have attempted to maintain a close liaison
with that organization ever since. I have been, on occasion,
both uplifted by courageous positions taken on particular issues by the N.E.A. and relatively disheartened by the lack of
any stand at all on certain of the other burning issues of our
times.

Like many other powerful lobby, a teacher's organization

can be an immensely valuable force for ethical and social change. The direction of the organization depends entirely upon the courage of its members. Rather than leaving the organization work to others, whom many of us then comfortably condemn, it seems to me it is our obligation to do our best to *shape* the tone and values of an organization that both protects and oftentimes befriends us.

It is not in the nature of a large, well-financed and politically established organization to set out to subvert or even to excoriate that larger social system of which it has come to be an instrumental and important part. Individual members of the unions, on the other hand, need not be restricted by these familiar institutional restraints. Free-thinking teachers, rank and file members of the N.E.A. and A.F.T., constantly rebel, stand up for moral and political issues and address such matters of conscience as the cumulative record, I.Q. testing, historical distortions and evasions, with all possible courage and integrity. It is precisely these free thinkers and iconoclastic souls (those who annoy and frequently infuriate their colleagues and administrators most) who will redeem the teacher unions in the eye of history.

There *is* a role for independent teachers in both of the teacher unions, but it is not the habitual function of the building representative or collector of the dues. Their role is one of counterfoil and voice of protest in the heart of the machine (at least where there is any chance at all to win the members over to a strong position on a matter of fair play) and, overall, the task of toiling always from within, not so much in order to win power or position, but rather in order to be able to exert some leverage on the ones who *do*.

In certain cities, states and national regions, the union leadership itself has been effectively and democratically won over by a number of strong and enterprising teachers of the kind who, in most other communities, are forever in the caucus that protests the policies and actions that the leadership supports. The situation often seems more fluid in the N.E.A., but this is not the same in every state and, on this score, my own view certainly is not impartial. Both groups now are changing far too fast to be able to predict two years ahead.

There is a different road, however, that many teachers have begun to take in recent years: one which relegates the large-scale national battles of the major unions to a second or third place. Thousands of embattled and impatient classroom teachers are beginning, more and more, to invest their energies at the local level—and to do so through the vehicle of entirely new varieties of organizing instruments. I have in mind the interesting phenomenon of "teacher centers" which have begun to spring up with extraordinary speed during the period from 1975 to 1980.[26]

I have visited approximately fifteen of these centers—in New Haven, New York City, Milwaukee, Minneapolis, Chicago, San Francisco, Portland and Seattle. Each center I have seen is slightly different from the next. Some place major emphasis on teachers helping teachers in the areas of specific classroom skills. Others place greater emphasis on politics and mutual support for teachers who are in embattled situations. Some of the centers are operated as commercial ventures, although on a very modest scale. Many have union backing. A few have government funds. Whatever their origin or sponsorship, almost all of the teacher centers I have seen are nourished, above all, by a political commitment that is neither bureaucratic nor commercial.

Everyone who works within a typical teacher center does not have the same objectives. Nonetheless, in almost every center, there is an undertone of ethical/political conviction which appears to have been able to survive even the most reactionary moments of the mid-1970s, using the cover of curriculum development and teacher training for what, in effect, were predominantly political, partisan and grass-roots struggles. Although I've seen less than two dozen of these centers, I believe that there must be at least two hundred teacher centers now in operation coast to coast.

How do these centers start? Some, as we have seen, are begun with government or union funds or else by charitable private groups. More frequently, a group of teachers on their own will find a storefront in a low-rent neighborhood, stock it with a coffee maker, telephone, ditto machine—then churn out leaflets to distribute at a union meeting or in front of local schools. Before long, thirty or forty teachers start to drop in after school, mainly to relax, sip coffee and exchange ideas. Sometimes teachers will put in an old refrigerator and fill it with a case of beer.

Teacher centers are often able to raise government or foundation funds by placing emphasis on purely pedagogic matters such as reading workshops. Nonetheless, their real significance, so far as organization is concerned, lies in the power of the group to take away the fear and isolation in which so many teachers are compelled to work and live. A number of those teacher centers which began with only forty-five or fifty teachers from a handful of adjacent schools have rapidly grown to several hundred members when the word began to spread to teachers in surrounding rural and suburban towns.

The centers can offer more than coffee, beer and solidarity to isolated teachers. They can also provide the base for a political defense, a legal battle on behalf of teachers who are threatened with retaliation for the views which they espouse, access to defense attorneys and fund-raising lists, in order to be able to provide (first) quick advice, then serious counsel in the case of a protracted fight.

When wisely planned, these centers reach out also, beyond the teachers, to the sympathetic parents whom some of those teachers have begun to know, then to older students who have also felt a sense of friendliness and trust. Several centers have made strenuous efforts to involve, as well, the school custodi-

ans and secretaries. Often ignored by teachers in their organizing efforts, these are people who can wield substantial
power in a lot of public schools, especially those in which the
principal is absent from the building a great deal—or where
the principal is frequently distracted from the daily operations
of the school.

In situations of this kind, a friendly secretary often is the
sole determinant of whether the books a teacher orders for
September are available when class begins—or else do not
show up within the classroom until Christmas. School custodians who have made friends with the teachers, and who have
been respected as their equal and responsible co-workers,
often will come into a class at end of school, notice that we
have had to do a painting workshop on makeshift materials
since the year's allotment of manila paper has run out, will
disappear into a basement closet and return with several
reams of crisp but (up to now) well-hidden cardboard.

All of our co-workers, whether they are school custodians or
the people who prepare and serve our students' lunch each
day, ought to command respect for difficult and tedious work
well done. There is also the fact that any teacher who is fighting to transform the schools, and to subvert a number of un-
fortunate attitudes that most of us have been indoctrinated to
respect, will need to find all of the allies we can get. Here, as
in all other situations of potential confrontation in the public
schools, the goal of reaching out to people whom we frequently ignore, or just pass by, seems to me both ethical and
self-protective.

When parents, students, secretaries, school custodians and
teachers all begin to stop in at the same church basement on
a Friday afternoon, or for a potluck supper Friday night, principals also may begin to feel a little discontent at having been
left out. One center that I know begins the year by urging
local principals to stop in for a beer. If the invitation has been
made in earnest and good feeling, it is frequently accepted.

Neighborhoods differ so much in every city, and in every state, that no one can sensibly predict what kinds of coalitions will be possible in any given case. The organizational process needs to be adapted with intelligence and sophistication to every possibility of conceivable alliance. The purpose at all moments ought to be political. The goal is to win allies for a time of trouble—a time when people will discover the necessity of choosing sides.

If the teacher center limits itself to little more than cardboard carpentry and innovative games upon an innovative floor, then it will not be significant in forging allies for beleaguered teachers. If the center is political right from the start, however, it will almost automatically become the center of the rebel camp. Parents, teachers and other school employees will consider it their own home base.

It would be naive to argue that the teacher center represents an ideal, incorruptible—or even consistently ethical—center for the energies of teachers in rebellion. Ironically, indeed, the more they succeed, in terms of drawing larger and larger numbers, of forming links, liaisons and collaborations and obtaining government grants, the less they are likely to maintain their grass-roots flavor and their independent and indignant tone.

So I do not describe the teacher center here as if it were the sole solution or the best solution or the ultimate solution for those rebel teachers in pursuit of strength in numbers and collective power to uphold their aspirations and defend their dreams. I view these centers, rather, as one type of organization which, if faithful to their members and responsive to their own initial reason for existence, ought to be able to serve a special function at the local level which neither of the larger organizations can so easily uphold.

The teacher's job is dreadfully difficult, unprestigious, ill-rewarded. The lot of the rebel and independent-minded teacher is more difficult still. Perhaps the teacher center is a stage, a tendency, a clue to new directions, rather than a sufficient instrument for teacher action in itself.

Viewed in this spirit, and with these reservations, it is a cheerful and auspicious step on an uncharted road—one which, for thousands of American teachers, has been all too lonely, all too long.

4

Broadening Our Base:
Building Loyalty Between
the Teacher and the Class

A final stage in the creation of the coalition I propose is one which draws into its realm the students, along with the parents and the teachers, of the public schools.

In the situation of the parents, as opposed to that of their own children, there is seldom any real alternative to active organizing at a distance from the school itself. This is, in part, because of the limited time that parents have at their disposal, but also because the school mystique seems most impressive and imposing to those people (parents) who have been exposed to it only at erratic intervals—or only years before. The parents, therefore, tend to be least open to the process of demystification of the public school while they are making one of their infrequent visits.

The situation of their children is quite often the reverse. First of all, we do not need to search for them at home since we already find them in the classroom. More to the point, their daily participation in the rituals of public school enables them to scrutinize those rituals more critically than parents who come rarely to the school and, when they do, too often do so in a state of mind that is still clouded by the aura of a sanctified institution.

I do not mean by this that students come to the moment of desanctifying school by their own genius or good luck. With students as with parents, teachers need to take a conscious role in stripping away some of those tapestries of pretense and illusion that hang from the classroom walls.

Apart from the actions that have been described in the first section of this book, other specific actions on the part of teachers that will help to lessen and subvert the mystification of the school include a willingness to undercut the grading system and the tracking system, to confront head-on the multiple modes of sex discrimination in a public school, to join in plans contrived to win our students license to do independent work outside of school and in this way to undercut the school attendance rules. (Many teachers have succeeded in providing cover for well-motivated kids who have already mastered the essential areas of basic skills and obviously can profit from a semi-independent learning situation.)

In certain schools, the issues will be substantially different from the ones I have described: bilingual classes, test scores, improper use of psychiatric testing, child control by use of drugs without parent permission. In a ghetto neighborhood where the schools have often been most blatantly destructive, teachers do not need to struggle long to build a sense of solidarity with students. One teacher, for example, confronted with the common situation of a class of all-black children plagued with substitute teachers and with consequently hopeless reading scores for three years in a row, recounts the following sequence of events:

In one of the first days of her first week in the school, she speaks to the children of the situation in which they find themselves. She tells them, without hesitation, that they are in trouble. "Most students your age are just about three years ahead of you by now. Unless you work seriously and struggle hard to make up for the years that you have lost, you'll soon be pushing brooms—or pushing dope—or scrubbing floors for rich white people like the ones who run or who control these schools."

None of this, she says, has been their fault. They have been cheated by an unjust institution—one, she explains, which is not a mistake ("a slip-up") but which exists in order to create a class of powerless poor people.

She tells the students that they will never have a chance of getting out from under, so long as they wait for someone else to come and set them free. The teacher's objective, in her choice of words, is to begin, right from the first, to build a sense of just denunciation and, more than that, a *lever* of denunciation in each child's mind: something to fight for, a cause they can uphold, a visible enemy, and good reasons to support their teacher in a struggle to transcend enormous odds.

It is the truth that all of these kids have been mistreated by the public schools. They *are* at war. So, too, is every student in this nation, although—in the cosmetic setting of suburban schools—the war remains forever undeclared.

The teacher's primary goal, in this particular case, is to identify some drastic and dramatic means by which to rid the classroom of its deathlike mood. The room is morbid, full of chalk dust and stale air, intermingled with the smell of floor wax, gathered and accreted in the course of ninety years. The windows, for some reason, are nailed shut. She pulls the nails and flings the windows open. A smell of lilac from a nearby garden drifts into the room.

The students, if not universally elated, are all at least attentive to her words. She promises the class that she will soon bring in a lot of paint and posters to cheer up the walls. She promises, too, that she will bring her record player the next day.

It is at this point that she also starts to build the groundwork for her own professional protection. She tells the students of her serious concern regarding the risks and obstacles at stake, not only for them but for herself as well, especially in outside interference from the school administration: "We will be doing certain things that are not really wanted in this school. The reason we will do them is in order to fight back against a system that has been unfair."

Her goal, at this point, is to be certain that the students will play ball and will assist her in a multitude of ways that might be crucial for her own survival. She sets out on a brief discussion with the class, in order to establish some of the most important means by which a class is judged to be "unruly" or else "well-behaved."

The instant consensus of the class is stated in five simple words: *filing quietly in the stairs.*

If some of this appears a little crazy to the reader, especially the reader who is unfamiliar with the daily rituals of public school, few students will find it difficult to understand. There are certain items that are close to sacrosanct within a well-run public school. To file quietly ("just like little soldiers," as the saying goes) is the clearest evidence of a properly soul-broken class.

The day after the teacher speaks of this, her students line up elegantly beside the door, wait for her signal and then file to the stairs—with all the discipline of William Calley's soldiers marching to My Lai. Next day, the second-grade teacher makes a sudden appearance at the classroom door. The children jump to their feet, turn eyes right to the teacher and recite in unison: "Good morning, Miss McCall!"

A smile is fixed and frozen on her jaw: "What well-behaved and cultivated children!" She turns to the teacher to explain why she has come to pay a call. "I want you to know—your children are the talk of the whole school! Everyone is so well impressed. *The way they have been filing in the stairs!*"

The students stare straight at their teacher (the teacher stares right back) as Miss McCall goes out the door. From that day on, for six or seven weeks, there is not one intrusion from outside.

Even at this point, nonetheless, there is a still more challenging issue to confront. The most difficult job is not to win the solidarity of students, but to get across the message to the class that—lilac blossoms and fresh air aside—they soon will be asked to work at an incredibly hard pace.

She tells the pupils that hard work doesn't need to be unpleasant and might even be exciting if they feel the willingness and determination to collaborate with some of her ideas. She also says they will not need to bother with Scott Foresman readers, nor with that invidious orange box from S.R.A. After all of this, she says once more, they have to get themselves prepared to do some tough, consecutive lessons in the weeks ahead. If not, everything else that they have tried to do will probably be lost.

In view of the sense of common cause and of embattled struggle which she has constructed by this time, the students respect her words and do not try to play games with her confidence and trust. They study with devotion (students teaching one another in spare moments) in order to try to make up for so many lost years. The children are excited by the sense of shared conspiracy with one another, and with their teacher too, in order to guarantee their own survival. They work as if they now have joined together in some sort of pedagogic "forced march." There is a goal to reach, an evil system to undo, and any number of dragons to destroy. The sense of struggle and of concrete goals (math, reading and writing, ethics and the power to transform) soon becomes intense and credible. It is upon this recognition of dead-earnest combat that all the rest of what the children and the teacher soon will do is going to depend.

All of the above is based upon a situation of extreme and visible exploitation which the pupils recognize right from the start. Teachers in the suburbs often make the point that very little of the blatant chaos and overt discrimination of a ghetto school is present in a rich, relatively stable and superficially "successful" public school. The overriding function of political indoctrination is, however, virtually unchanged.

If teachers can establish this preliminary point, and if we then can demonstrate the multiple ways in which it takes effect, we are—from that point on—in a position to establish strong alliances with pupils, both in rich suburban neighborhoods and in the poorest rural neighborhoods or ghetto slums. All students in an unjust social order are the victims, though they are not equal victims, of a twelve-year sequence of oppression and deceit. They are all victims of a pedagogic structure built on lies.

5

Short-Term Goals and Long-Term Victories

The four preceding chapters place almost exclusive emphasis on the ways by which to reach those three essential groups that can create a viable coalition for a teacher's self-defense in time of crisis.

What is a plausible sequence of events that might lead up to a crisis of the kind I have in mind? Imagine a young and highly competent—but temporary—teacher who is offended by the political bias of the texts and other materials in the classrooms of the school. He starts to bring in a number of unauthorized books and other forms of documentation on his own. The principal hears about the teacher's actions, warns the teacher for the sake of his career to work more closely within acceptable bounds, but two months later is obliged by pressure from the school board to issue a more formal admonition. He also forbids the teacher to continue meeting with the people in the nearby neighborhood. The teacher refuses to give in—and is dismissed. The union refuses to intervene because the teacher has not yet become a member.

The teacher turns to the parents for support.

A logical scenario, from this point on, might start with something very simple and routine such as a letter to the principal and school board, signed by parents, a number of pupils, a handful of teachers—and requesting a public hearing in ten days.

If, by the date requested, there has been no answer, subsequent actions might include a sequence of this sort: (1) A modest delegation of parents and students pays a visit to the school board, asking in polite terms for a prompt, responsible hearing. (2) A larger delegation pays a *second* visit, stating in less gentle terms a firm demand for an immediate hearing. (3) If this demand should be ignored, or if the hearing is indefinitely postponed, then it is perhaps the moment for the group to find a lawyer and for the lawyer to proceed to file suit. The lawyer requests a hearing on the part of both of the teacher who has been dismissed and of those parents who, in recognition of the teacher's loyalty and hard work, feel defrauded of their children's rights to decent education. (4) Simultaneous with the filing of legal papers, there might be a formal presentation to the press. (5) At the same moment that the grievance of one teacher is addressed, parents might seize the chance to raise some of those other issues which this situation only symbolizes. (6) Before, during and pursuant to the court case, constant meetings might be held to galvanize and to extend support in order to exploit whatever public controversy is created. (7) Lawyers, in the presentation of this case, ought to be raising certain of the larger issues at every point where legal process or the judge's patience will allow. (8) Prior even to a final outcome in the courts, plans should be in process for the type of public actions which will capitalize, in every way conceivable, upon a legal victory—or else to plan for extralegal tactics in the event the case is lost and an appeal is lost as well.

It goes without saying that it takes a specific crisis of real drama and significance before the total sequence I've described here can begin. If there is no issue both substantial and dramatic in appeal, neither legal action nor attention from the press is of much worth. Many groups are able to *provoke* a crisis if they do not find one handed to them in advance. Most often, however, school boards or school principals, even if they do not dare to do something so extreme as to dismiss a popular teacher, will do at least a few things so irrational and so absurd as to present us with the cause, or causes, that inspire both a protest action and a legal case as well.

The challenge is seldom how to find an issue. It is to know the way to *use* one. This is not possible, to start with, if we cannot find a lawyer who is willing to collaborate with the interests of the coalition. This can often be a controversial point with certain lawyers. Those who feel we live in an essentially just and democratic social system will not wish to use the courtroom to advance a cause; their sole desire is to win the case. This is the kind of lawyer we must carefully avoid.

The lawyer we need is one who tries very hard to win the case on its own merits but also struggles to provide a legal, extra-legal and political education to the public through the process of the trial and through statements in the press.

Lawyers who refuse to do this often speak of the client's interest as their sole concern. Frequently, however, they are thinking mainly of their own, recognizing a potential loss of business or acceptance by their peers if they should manage to offend the court. These are the kinds of lawyers who will often warn a client that he or she is being "used" by agitators for extraneous objectives. ("You're being naive. You're being used by other people.") The goals appear extraneous, of course, only because this type of lawyer feels that saving one man's or one woman's job, as well as helping to advance his own career, is more important than assisting in the build-up of an organization for the long-term transformation of the schools.

Having been through this problem with a number of friends in several situations, I have learned how skillfully a basically conventional attorney can persuade a client to pursue his or her own selfish ends at the expense of those whose efforts won that person legal counsel in the first place.

Even beyond the sticky question of which lawyer to employ,

and once the type of lawyer that we need has been retained, a second challenge is the designation of two separate goals, both of which we must pursue at the same time, but by two parallel roads. One goal is to achieve a victory within the courts. (If we sacrifice this purpose altogether, then those critics who believe that we are only using someone for extraneous goals are possibly correct.) The long-term goal, however, is to build a sense of heightened strength among the parents, teachers, students—sometimes maverick school officials—who provide us with support and who, in turn, are counting on the public interest which this case elicits to broaden their numbers and to reinforce the sense of confidence within their ranks.

Attorneys who will fight a case, not just to win an immediate victory but also to create a forum for discussion of important issues, may very well offend the courtroom protocol of decorous and old-fashioned lawyers—but they are not the ones who are naive. It is the conventional lawyer (the one who turns us down) who proves himself naive. He is naive because he does not know the reason why we worked so hard to bring this case to trial from the start.

In the event that readers are uncertain as to what I have in mind in speaking of "specific" legal cases, I would like to offer four examples. In at least three of these four examples, plaintiffs have at times won landmark victories.

One of them concerns the issue of the flag pledge, mentioned earlier. As we have seen, the Supreme Court has already found the forcible imposition of the pledge to be unconstitutional. Since the pledge is seldom *viewed* as voluntary in the public schools, and almost never treated as a casual matter, it would appear that many principals and school boards have been operating in defiance of the law.

Teachers who intend to fight this issue in a state or federal court are protected by precedent, as well as by their civil rights, against all forms of top-down condemnation or abuse;

yet very few teachers, fewer parents and scarcely any student I have ever met in public school are cognizant of the precedents in question. This, then, is an ideal legal issue to fulfill both short-term purposes and long-term goals.

Another legal struggle—specific in its detail, long term in its results—is one that can be built upon another issue which has been discussed above: the release of test scores, records, teacher comments and psychological exams that fill the cumulative records of the public schools. Here again, although state laws may vary on the details of this point, federal law demands the full divulgence of such records.

In spite of the law, as we have seen, schools tend to employ a number of devices of intimidation to deny the parents full and open access to these records. Teachers who take the action I suggest—of opening such records to the parents and the students of their school—can fight a good strong battle in defense of their behavior if a school board should object.

A third area in which it seems possible, ethical and correct to launch a tough, aggressive public battle is the one, described above, of our approach to history. Any school board dumb enough to try to punish or suppress a teacher for the honest presentation of the views of Helen Keller or Thoreau, will find itself in an extremely weak position in a court of law. Here again, although the legal issue would be worth the courtroom battle in itself, the larger possibilities—in terms of public scrutiny of school-mandated lies—are more important still.

A fourth and final example is one that has already been attempted and, to some degree, proven successful. This is the matter of initiation of individual or class-action suits against school districts, or specific school boards, for consumer fraud. The central issues here are virtually the same as those that would be raised in any other suit based on consumer fraud. Those who fear that they cannot win this type of suit in terms such as those which have been raised in the first section of this book ("ethical deception" on the part of public schools) may use instead an issue which can far more easily be proven in a court of law: the school's default in areas of basic skills.

If less important in political respects than the larger point of school indoctrination, the issue of skills is easier to argue, since the case can be presented in the same terms that the school boards claim to value and respect: tests and test scores, reading skills, math levels and the like. Once the case is in the court and in the public eye, the deeper points about historical distortion and political indoctrination can be brought into the limelight as we like and in the ways we choose.

The issue of "school as a consumer fraud" has already caught the eye of high officials in the nation's capital—and, in particular, of George McGovern. A number of high school graduates, McGovern said in an interesting U.S. Senate speech delivered on September 8, 1978, "refuse to forget what they did not learn in school. Recently a high school student of normal intelligence sued his school in San Francisco for educational malpractice—he had been awarded a diploma even though he could read only at a fifth-grade level." Attorneys for various state Offices of Education, said McGovern, "agree that the number of such suits will increase, and that increasingly they will succeed."[27]

There is one point in all of this that seems sufficiently important to restate one final time: None of these legal battles is significant, in the long run, if we do not hold ourselves in readiness to move beyond the realm of law in the event that legal avenues should fail to work. This is the reason why most groups that are experienced in struggles of this kind do not restrict their efforts to the narrow parameters of legal issues, but work at all times to make preparations for more passionate forms of struggle later on.

These forms of extra-legal struggle, and the ways that we make use of press and public information to advance our cause, are highly controversial even within the ranks of strong, political and unintimidated people. The reason for controversy is the fact that public actions which transcend the limits of the law will often lose us significant portions of our earlier support. There are times, however, when a teacher or a group of parents and teachers have no option but to forfeit a certain portion of their backing in order to invest their faith and energy in an action that affords some chance of victory.

Nothing is won without the risk of payment of a price, even if it is no more than the loss of friendships in pursuit of ethical ideals. Nothing that counts as much as this is ever won for free.

6

Creating a Crisis— or Awaiting One

A legal case is a crisis in itself. Often, however, there is no single issue so specific as to justify legal action. In situations like these, many parent-and-teacher groups are likely to sit, complain, and wait for months—or even years—before an incident occurs to constitute a crisis.

People with a just cause, but no concrete and dramatic issue, need not wait forever if they have the willingness to force the issue on their own. It remains, at almost all times, within the power of a group of serious and determined people to provoke a crisis of the kind they need, and at the time they want, so long as they know the issue is for real and so long as the crisis—though "provoked"—is not "contrived."

In one respect, our customary inclination not to force an issue, but to sit and wait for an important issue to occur, is very much in keeping with the passive sense of those who view themselves as objects of historic process, never the progenitors of change. Teachers who grew addicted to the catchcries of the 1960s often speak, in perfect jargon, of "awaiting the correct conditions" or "objective situation" for an action or a protest of whatever kind. If, by this, they mean no more than to make realistic surveys of the power they possess, in proportion to the goals that they pursue, there is no question but that this would be a sane and proper caution.

If, however, as too often is the case, they simply are waiting for the school board or the school administration to provide them with the issues (the "conditions") to inspire an important struggle, then it seems to me that they have abdicated too much power and have permitted those whom they oppose to set the terms, and even choose the time, when they will be allowed to fight.

In many situations in the past few years, parents have known, long in advance, that a dismissal or a non-renewal was quite clearly in the air for one of the outspoken teachers in their school. The school board, as of June, however, had not yet discussed the teacher's case. As a result, no one spoke up in his or her defense. Two months later, in the deep heat of August, a summary dismissal of the teacher went through school committee session in ten minutes on a quiet Tuesday night. Students were gone. The teacher centers had been closed down for vacation. Half of the vocal parents did not even hear of the dismissal until after Labor Day.

The ritual of midsummer non-renewal occurs so frequently nowadays that we should take it as a challenge to ourselves to sniff out serious issues long before the hour is too late and to force these issues at a time when we have power to respond. Those who wait for "the correct conditions" to initiate a just and ethical demand will often wait forever.

If it takes a catalytic action of a certain reasonable kind in order to incite a school board to commit a reckless and precipitous deed, then it seems to me it is for us to choose with care the day we act, how many or how few should be involved, in just which schools, and at what grades or in which neighborhoods.

This is not an invitation to cause needless trouble in a relatively decent school which has the luck to work beneath the supervision of a loyal and protective principal. It is rather common, in the course of struggles that take place in public schools, that people tend to turn the soonest against those school officials who appear most vulnerable and open: vulnerable not because they have been stupidly oppressive, but rather because they have been candid with us and have tried their best to be our friends. (Blacks, in anger, will sometimes strike, in the first burst of fury, at those whites who work in close companionship right at their sides, solely because they are the only representatives of the white race within easy reach.)

Whatever the context, common sense ought to direct us to attempt to spare a sympathetic principal or other school official, especially when we know that almost every educational system in this nation has in its employ so many other individuals who do deserve and oftentimes invite a knock-down struggle. As an overall rule, it seems to me that practical rebels ought to do their best to treat with great respect even half-hearted allies.

One other point might possibly be misconstrued unless I clarify my words a bit. The purpose that I have in mind is not to see if we can cause a fellow teacher, or ourselves, to get thrown out—purely for the sake of offering our friends and allies a dramatic cause. Any behavior of this sort is, at the least, perverse and self-defeating. A decent teacher who survives for fifteen years is fifteen times more useful than a decent but impatient martyr who survives for only one. Our purpose is not to court dismissal but to be sufficiently alert to recognize a moment when dismissal is most likely to occur. If that moment is so timed as to deny us power to defend ourselves, then I believe that teachers are employing excellent sense by making certain that they are the ones to force the school board to take action. If it's certain to happen, and we know it's going to happen, why should we sit and wait when we can be the ones who *make* it happen, and can do so at a time of our own choice, when we are in a good position to fight back?

In the heat of struggle, as we have seen, many people tend to recognize no other goal than a specific victory in the immediate case at hand. Others understand that there are larger purposes as well. All of this brings us back to an idea discussed in the preceding chapter: the tactical distinction between a short-term purpose and a long-term goal.

The short-term goal will be essential to provoke discussion and to gather followers for a particular struggle. The long-term goal is crucial if the struggle is not going to be over once that single issue has been won. A coalition, for example, that intends to fight the issue of renewal of a teacher's contract may, if it likes, speak only of the teacher under fire or it can focus instead on hiring practices as a whole. In the same sense, in a rent strike, organizers can fight hard against the landlord to see immediate needs relieved within one building for one year; but if they do not emphasize as well, and finally demand, a written promise of a set of concrete follow-ups for all the buildings owned by this one landlord, and with guarantees for several years to come, they will be forced to undergo the same ordeal one winter later.

In all of these cases, the battle can be fought on the short-term issue only. A clear reiteration of the larger problem guarantees instead that no one will be silenced by a single court decision or a single calculated instance of capitulation from the school administration. The moment of victory, in situations which are carefully prepared, leads us instantly to resurrect the larger point which this one situation only symbolizes. Instead of ending an important effort, it helps to lay the groundwork for the next one.

If we do not keep in mind considerations of this kind, then it remains, for those who like, to let us think that we have won a victory when they know well that they will win the war. The point is that, without extravagant rhetoric but with some definite connections being drawn between immediate issues and large over-arching goals, we can both win the victory *and* launch the war.

It is hard enough to organize and to construct a coalition. It is harder still to reconstruct one from the ground up. It is not so hard to keep a cause in motion, once it has begun. The strategy of the school board is most frequently to give us enough, in one particular case, to send us home with the idea that we have won all that we hoped for. If we are wise, we will not let our adversaries send us home to bed "right after supper." Instead, we will be putting our heads together to anticipate the next ten battles that will lead not just to our own personal vindication but to a victory for every child and for every teacher in the system.

7

Confronting the Press and TV: Dissemination of the Facts

Nothing we do will have much impact on the consciousness of other people if we do not work out certain methods of dissemination of the facts themselves. This process runs the full range of promotion and publicity, from production and distribution of a neighborhood newsletter to the composition of a press release.

For many people, the following information may appear self-evident. For those who have never had any dealings with the press, some of this may prove to be of help. An initial consideration, in most cases, is to attempt to isolate a single journalist whom we believe to be open, or most likely to be open, to the cause that we uphold. Even in states or cities where the press appears to be alarmingly conservative, teachers are often able to pin down a handful of reporters who are sympathetic to their goals.

The best example is one that I recall from the Southwest. Here, a city editor and good reporter have been able to turn out and get into print so much first-rate material which, apart from all else, is well-written copy as to place the owners of the paper in a difficult position. It would hurt the circulation of the paper to dismiss them. Political organizers, liberal readers, poor folks in the Spanish-speaking and Mestizo barrios, learn to be quite certain to give all releases, stories and exclusives only to this writer. She, in turn, is careful to submit her story only on the nights when her co-worker is on duty.

This is, however, an exceptional situation. The usual method of dissemination of a story is through the preparation of a press release. One familiar format for a press release starts out with a short phrase which describes the content, then is followed by a date, identification of those who have released the story, and "phone for further contact." The statement itself, which might not get a great deal of attention if it's longer than two pages, should (like the headline) represent an effort on our part to write the story for the journalist or for the editor. If it's done well, even a very good reporter sometimes does no more than to revise its sequence, cut it to size, insert some extra data (comments from the opposition, for example) and then send it to the press.

No news release, no matter how well written, is likely to make it into print if it is not real news. No item is news if it does not have time value of some sort. A general story of the poor conditions in an urban public school is not considered news—except perhaps for an essay in a Sunday magazine or in a weekly feature section. If, however, the abysmal situation of one public school can be described, in vivid terms, as part and parcel of a genuine news story ("Students Close Down High School Cafeteria: Protest Unsanitary Preparation"), then it is possible to offer to reporters an ideal package of real news and of important background at the same time.

Even the most responsive journalists are likely to lose interest right away if what they see appears to them as "just the same old story" about ineffective public schools. If they can write instead that a group of fifty high school students, joined by kitchen volunteers, five teachers and two dozen parents, have forced the school board to agree to schedule hearings on health dangers in the school, then the details cease to be mere repetition but an item of good reading—what some editors, however hostile, may identify as a story that belongs on the front page.

Just as important as the production of a press release is its effective distribution. First we must find a handful of reliable co-workers who will keep their automobiles available, especially when the group is working frantically against the clock, ready to deliver the release to each newspaper and to every radio and TV station. (The delivery ought to be in early evening if we hope to make the morning papers, 11 A.M. or thereabouts to make the evening paper and the TV news.)

Assuming that there are no particular writers whom we know and trust, the best alternative is to get hold of the names of certain liberal or open-minded contact people at each TV station or newspaper. The least effective method is simply to leave a press release to sit and gather cobwebs in a crowded press-room, in a shallow metal basket on a messy desk, a few feet from the editor's left elbow. It is likely to remain there all night long.

Of all conventional methods to get out the news, a press conference is certainly the most dramatic. In this situation, an effort first is made to hook reporters on the story, whether by phone or by a "tentative release," thereby to get them all together in a single room and, at a single moment, to give out the details of the story to everyone at once.

Two documents are needed in advance of a press conference. One is a brief, intriguing statement that provides no details other than the place, the time and possibly one or two important high-points of the story. (To deliver the statement with all possible details spelled out in advance is to be reasonably certain that there will be no one present at the conference.) The second necessary document is, of course, the press release itself, which is to be read at the press conference.

Another detail, often helpful in creating a good press conference, is to settle on two or three people to present the case for the entire group. This way, journalists cannot resort to a device they otherwise may use to great effect: namely, to ask a lot of members of our group a similar question and then to make a major point out of the slight divergences between our answers.

Once a press release is read, and once the basic point has been presented clearly for the TV cameras, many people emphasize that we should take care not to let reporters lead us off in ten or twenty new directions of their own. Those who do this can quote exclusively the answers to their questions—and ignore all that we had hoped to say. The strategy, on our side, is to answer an irrelevant question with a statement that, in fact, does little more than to repeat the gist of what we said before.

A final approach, used frequently by politicians at all levels, is to give a "leak"—or an "exclusive"—just before a major paper goes to press, soon enough so they can get it into print, late enough so that other reporters still will feel impelled to come to the press conference and not regard the story as outdated matter. The sole reason to do this is, of course, to get a special favor in return—the likelihood of sympathetic treatment, for example, or a promise of conspicuous attention.

A last-minute conversation with one major paper in my city, five years back, was instrumental in achieving an effective front-page story, yet its release was so close to the time of the press conference that this did not keep the other media representatives away. Often, moreover, a conspicuous story in the written press provides the bait for better attention in the TV news. News, in this respect, repeatedly "creates news."

So much of this chapter deals with the large picture—press relations and TV—that I would like to conclude by coming back to the grass roots. In the long run, all the press, TV and radio attention in the city, state or nation will prove to be useless if we do not build a strong and loyal core of parents, kids and teachers at the start. There is no substitute for hard, exhausting organization of this kind.

The use of door-to-door approaches to entire strangers by a paired team (parent and teacher, if possible), accumulation and continual updating of a set of contact cards with numbers and addresses for both work and home, the use of fliers and newsletters mailed to parents or just handed out to kids (not by a teacher) at the end of school, the endless use of phone calls for last-minute checks so people won't forget a crucial meeting they have planned and promised to attend, the evolution of an instant "telephone tree" by which one person calls three others, and those others each call three—all of these efforts constitute the only possible basis for the long-term loyalty and mutual confidence that can endure beyond a single week, or month, or year.

None of this, I'm sure, will lead us to a pedagogic revolution. Nor, to use a term that I first used in chapter one, will it turn the system upside down or inside out. What it will do, however, is to give us the first taste of battle and the confidence that, in the last event, determined people, working together, can do more than merely to join their hands in struggle, but can labor long with tact and skill, and persevere in face of problems of all kinds, and now and then can even overcome these obstacles and struggle on a little more—and ultimately know the taste of vctory.

8

Fear of Victory: Dangers of the Numbers Game

Various obstacles to any real success in organizing appear so vivid and so obvious as to constitute almost a set of incantations, neon lights and admonitions to remind us of the pitfalls in our way.

Most obvious is the inclination of many energetic organizers to exhaust themselves through internecine quarrels long before we ever come to grips with our real opposition. Often it seems that we forget the very name and nature of the unjust apparatus that we labor to transform, long hours before we ever get to anything like head-on confrontation—because we have expended so much of our energy in combat with each other.

Another inheritance from many misguided struggles of the past is an inclination to distrust our leaders, and to do our best (when we do make the tentative choice to trust some leaders for a time) to do what it takes to break them down as fast as possible—and then to drive them out. This is the case today in many parent-teacher coalitions. Natural leaders, as they gradually emerge, have been compelled to undergo intense harassment, seldom for their failures but more often for their most effective actions and their most audacious dreams. The label "ego trip" appears repeatedly within those fearful sessions of recrimination that so often represent the final chapter in the story of a once-vital coalition.

Teachers and parents—all of us, I think—have got to learn to separate the fear of domination from the fear of excellence. If any group I know, or one with which I work, is able to discover or to move up through its ranks a leader with the power, first to stand, and then to speak in the first person present, unafraid, both to denounce that system of deception and injustice which a public school now represents, then to announce a dream of justice he or she has both the will and the determination to make real, I hope we will have brains enough not to attempt to undercut the passion and the strength that person offers us.

All of the above seem to be symptoms of a single problem which is far too common in the effort to create long-lasting coalitions. I am thinking of an attitude—a mood—which I have heard described by one of my old friends as "a radical inclination toward the insufficient."

I think of it sometimes as the "Cult of Incompletion." It is that sort of laid-back state of mind that looks with scorn upon the need for strong, consistent and uninterrupted processes of work and aspiration, but makes a virtue rather of the interrupted venture, of the unsuccessful fight.

It is time for us to face this problem of our own inherent fear of strength head-on. I think that we should be prepared to strive with all our hearts to be strong teachers, efficacious adults, unintimidated leaders and strong-minded provocations in the consciousness of parents and within the lives of children too.

There are some authors who, for several years, have sought to make a virtue of the capability to start and stop things in response to sudden impulse. There is, with this, the strange phenomenon of those who undergo a kind of anguish at the likelihood of real success—as if effectiveness itself must henceforth (by association with the Pentagon or I.B.M.) carry the copyright of evil men. I see no reason why we need to choose between a contaminated sense of competence on the one hand and a benign sense of ineptitude on the other. Those who struggle to transform the public schools cannot afford the presence in their midst of people who choose to tamper with the lives of children, not for the sake of the children or the teachers, but rather to satisfy their own unconscious need for self-defeat.

A final point may be of use in organizing teachers, students, parents—or all three.

Imagine the situation of the teacher who has worked for weeks to get to know the parents in the neighborhood around the school, has worked hard with pupils in the class, and has made a number of efforts to build up a sense of solidarity with teachers—then finds, when an initial meeting has been called within the basement of a local church, that seven people finally appear. Teachers often tell me stories of this nature and, of course, they speak of their enormous disappointment every time.

Whenever groups of parents and teachers grow depressed at situations of this kind, it might be of use to give each other brief and optimistic history reminders. In 1955, Martin Luther King and Rosa Parks began the struggle for desegregation of an urban transportation system with no more than a few hundred trusted friends and organizers. Within five years, they had created a dynamic and effective movement that involved at least five hundred thousand people.

Another point, in reference to the anguish at low numbers which so many people feel, is that it simply doesn't take one hundred or two hundred people to prepare the groundwork for a grass-roots coalition. Often all it requires is a close and loyal few to build a core of people that is capable, when need demands, of reaching out to hundreds more. If a teacher with a grade-school class of twenty-eight or thirty-two is able to win the strong allegiance of no more than seven parents, and perhaps of no more than three teachers in a faculty of twenty-five, those numbers offer all it takes to galvanize another twenty teachers and two hundred parents more in serious struggle on behalf of any worthwhile and dramatic cause.

It is easy to forget, when counting heads, that a very small number of the parents in a neighborhood will ever have time to take a burning interest in on-going matters of this kind. If, then, in our number panic, we can quietly subtract ten or more who will not really care (or, more precisely, don't have time to care), then we can see that a substantial core of seven allies already starts to constitute almost one half of the committed parents in the class.

If, in addition to these, a teacher should also receive the backing of a larger organization like the chain of teacher centers I've described, and if (at least within the high schools) we can manage to build up some active and responsible support from even half-a-dozen students in the class, then right away that early core of only six or eight begins to represent the dedicated center of much larger numbers of committed people who already know each other from a series of suppers, seminars and such.

I often undergo a sudden sense of hopelessness at walking into a room and finding only half-a-dozen heads to count, in contrast to the thousands of people who appear at rallies on TV. Mass rallies serve a useful function at particular times and for quite special goals. One of these goals is *not* to organize the parents on the block, students in the classroom, teachers in the halls. Small steps, meticulously and consciously contrived, leading to small but loyal coalitions, appear to me to be the only means by which to organize the grass-roots basis for those long-term struggles which so many teachers seem prepared to undertake.

One revolution started with an unprepared tea party. Others start in mountain sanctuaries with the preparation of a military plan and with painstaking lessons in the way to oil and repair a gun. The revolution that we need to bring about within our public schools is one that will begin with someone—parent or teacher, child or adolescent, well-to-do or poor—quietly summoning up the nerve, then softly knocking on a neighbor's door.

Postscript:
"Written Under Protest"

William R. Tysseling
Attorney at Law
401 Clark Avenue
Ames, Iowa 50010

May 18, 1976

Mr. Don Carlson
Welch Junior High School
321 State Street
Ames, Iowa 50010

Dear Mr. Carlson:

Suzanne Chaplik and her parents have contacted me regarding Suzanne's participation in the Pledge of Allegiance at assemblies.

Suzanne relates that it has been required that she either:

1. stand during the Pledge of Allegiance at assemblies, or
2. bring a note from her parents requesting that this requirement be waived, this note to be maintained in her permanent record, or
3. that she author and submit a statement of her convictions, also to be included in a permanent record.

In an effort to resolve this matter, I would request two things. First, that you notify me of any inaccuracies in Suzanne's perceptions of these requirements and second, that you provide copies of the system or school policies with regard to the Pledge of Allegiance and the inclusion of such information in the permanent record.

Due to the time constraints of the end of the term. I would also request some response by Friday, May 21, 1976 in order that Suzanne might have this information before the assemblies scheduled for May 26 and May 27, 1976.

Thank you for your assistance and consideration in this matter.

> *Very truly yours,*
> *William R. Tysseling*

Mr. Don Carlson
Welch Junior High School
32 State Street
Ames, Iowa 50010

May 24, 1976

William R. Tysseling
Attorney at Law
401 Clark Avenue
Ames, Iowa 50010

Dear Mr. Tysseling:

I have received your letter requesting information about your client, Suzanne Chaplik, and her parents, participating in the Pledge of Allegiance at the Welch Junior High School assemblies.

We have followed the practice of opening the assemblies at Welch Junior High School with the Pledge of Allegiance for the past twelve years. All students are required to stand for this activity unless they have a written excuse from their parents requesting permission to remain seated during the Pledge of Allegiance. Students may also write a request for permission to remain quietly seated during this activity. However, their parents must sign this request.

It is accurate that these requests are maintained in the student's cumulative folder until the student changes his/her desire to participate in the Pledge of Allegiance or leaves junior high school, either by three years of completion or moves out of the district. At this time the note is removed and the fact of action that this student does not stand for the Pledge of Allegiance may be recorded.

Welch Junior High School does not have a written policy on the governance of the students participating in the Pledge of Allegiance. It is an activity that we use to help students gain a greater respect for the freedom and privileges we have in America and a sense of allegiance for which it stands. However, a written note requesting permission, signed by the student's parents, will exclude the students from the activity. We ask the parents to assume the responsibility for the junior high students, their children, in such a decision. We don't feel this type of decision should be based on a daily whim of a junior high student.

If you have other questions, please feel free to ask me. Hopefully this issue can be resolved by Suzanne and her parents working with the school.

Sincerely,
Don Carlson
Principal

William R. Tysseling
Attorney at Law
401 Clark Avenue
Ames, Iowa 50010

June 16, 1976

Ames School Board
and
Mr. David Moorhead
Superintendent of Schools
120 South Kellogg Avenue
Ames, Iowa 50010

Ladies and Gentlemen:

Suzanne Chaplik and her parents have asked me to pursue the issue of Suzanne's participation in the Pledge of Allegiance at Welch Junior High School assemblies.

Attached you will find correspondence including a letter dated May 18, 1976 to Don Carlson, Principal of Welch Junior High School, and a letter dated May 24, 1976 from Mr. Carlson in response, together with a statement of convictions submitted by Suzanne to Welch Junior High School.

In summary, Suzanne has been required to submit a statement of convictions together with a note from her parents which is to be maintained in her permanent file for the purpose of "excusing" her from standing for the Pledge of Allegiance.

Suzanne's position is twofold:

1. She cannot be required to stand for the Pledge of Allegiance.
2. Even if she could be required to do so, inclusion of any "excuse" from such activity cannot be maintained in her permanent record.

I believe these are both sound legal positions.

I believe this is a symbolic gesture protected by the First

Amendment and that inclusion in a permanent record of any
materials relating to a student's refusal to participate in the
Pledge of Allegiance can only be found to be an unconstitutional deterrent to the exercise of free speech. I believe that
the inclusion of any such notation also falls within the purview
of the "loyalty oath" cases of the Supreme Court, and would
also be found unconstitutional on these grounds.

I also question the appropriateness of such a requirement. It
seems anomalous that in attempting to teach students ". . . a
greater respect for the freedom and privileges we have in
America . . ." the schools should choose to abridge the First
Amendment freedoms and privileges guaranteed by the Con-
stitution.

I am also concerned with the teaching process in which the
parents of a junior high school student are asked to assume
responsibility for the student's decision making. The taking of
a student's right to self-determination over so symbolic an issue seems not to reflect a respect for freedom or to encourage
a sense of allegiance to a political and social nation but rather
to demonstrate the lack of such freedom and to unnecessarily
create a distaste and anger for political and social governance.

It is our request of the board and school administration that
no students be required to stand for the Pledge of Allegiance
and that no sanction, discrimination nor special treatment be
imposed upon those choosing not to stand.

Very truly yours,
William R. Tysseling

P.S. As a result of Suzanne's involvement in this matter it has
come to her attention that there are two separate files kept at
Welch Junior High School, one on curricular matters and another on discipline matters. While we do not resist the orderly
administration of such paperwork, it is a concern that upon

requesting to see their children's junior high school files, Suzanne's parents were not informed of the existence of the discipline folder.

While this may have been an oversight or previous to the creation of such files, we would ask that the matter be explored administratively and that in the future any parent or child requesting access to the files be informed of the existence of both.

WRT

Written Under Protest

This is a list of my convictions.
    It is written under protest.

I don't believe I need someone to
    write my words for my feeling.

I also believe that God is the only
    thing I can pledge myself to.

I strongly believe that standing for
    the pledge is also saying it.

If you were mute, you wouldn't say it
    by speaking but by standing.

I believe the pledge is truly contradictory
    to the actual state of the U.S.A.

Submitted by
Suzanne Chaplik
May 25, 1976

LIES

Telling lies to the young is wrong.
Proving to them that lies are true is wrong.
Telling them that God's in his heaven
and all's well with the world is wrong.
The young know what you mean. The young are people.
Tell them the difficulties can't be counted,
and let them see not only what will be
but see with clarity these present times.
Say obstacles exist they must encounter
Sorrow happens, hardship happens.
The hell with it. Who never knew
the price of happiness will not be happy.
Forgive no error you recognize,
it will repeat itself, increase,
and afterwards our pupils
will not forgive in us what we forgave.

Yevgeny Yevtushenko[28]

Appendix

Leads, Contacts, Publications

Education Groups and Publications devoted to Social and Pedagogic Change

Alternative Schools Network
1105 West Lawrence Avenue,
    Room 211
Chicago, Illinois 60604

The Center for Teaching and
    Learning
Box 8158, University Station
The University of North Dakota
Grand Forks, North Dakota
    58202

Community Education
275 Nineteenth Avenue
San Francisco, California, 94109

Council on Interracial Books
    for Children
1841 Broadway
New York, New York 10023

Education Exploration Center
P.O. Box 7339
Powderhorn Station
Minneapolis, Minnesota 55407

The Learning Center
2000 North Wells Street
Fort Wayne, Indiana 46808

Literacy Volunteers of America,
    Inc.
Midtown Plaza, Sixth floor
700 East Water Street
Syracuse, New York 13210

Laubach Literacy International,
    Inc.
1320 Jamesville Ave.
Box 131
Syracuse, NY 13210

National Coalition of
    Alternative Community Schools
1289 Jewett Street
Ann Arbor, Michigan 48104

National Institute of Education
Brown Building
Nineteenth and M Streets, N.W.
Washington, D.C. 20208

Pacific Region Association of
    Alternative Schools
1119 Geary Boulevard
San Francisco, California 94109

Public Education Association
20 West Fortieth Street
New York, New York 10018

Reading Reform Foundation
7054 East Indian School Road
Scottsdale, Arizona 85251

Rio Grande Education
    Association
P.O. Box 2241
Santa Fe, New Mexico 87501

World Education
1414 Sixth Avenue
New York, New York 10019

Hucksters in the Classroom (A study by Sheila Harty which reviews industry propaganda in schools). Published and distributed by the Center for Responsive Law, P.O. Box 19367, Washington, D.C., 20036. $20.00/year for corporations/$10.00/year for educators.

Inequality in Education. Published and distributed by The Center for Law and Education, Harvard University, 6 Appian Way, Cambridge, Massachusetts, 02139. Quarterly.$6.00/year.

Integrateducation: Race and Schools, Room 2220, University Library, University of Massachusetts, Amherst, Massachusetts, 01003. Bimonthly. $15.00/year.

Interracial Books for Children Bulletin. Published and distributed by the Council on Interracial Books for Children, C.I.B.C. Resource Center, 1841 Broadway, New York, New York, 10023. $15.00/year.

Politics and Education, Wesleyan Station, Fisk Hall, Middletown, Connecticut, 06457. Quarterly.$5.00/year.

Radical Teacher, published and distributed by the Center for the Study of Education and Politics, 285 Court Street, Middletown, Connecticut, 06457. Quarterly.$8.00/year.

TABS: Aides for Ending Sexism in School (Contains lesson plans, swap sections, posters, feature articles and reviews). 744 Carroll Street, Brooklyn, New York, 11215. Quarterly.$8.50/year.

The Testing Digest (A publication of The Project to DE-Mystify the Established Standardized Tests), 1129 Twenty-first Street, N.W., Washington, D.C., 20036. Quarterly.$4.00/year for students/ $12.00/year for institutions.

Working Teacher, c/o Working Teacher Educational Society, Box 46534, Postal Station G, 3760 West Tenth Avenue, Vancouver, B.C., V6R 4G8. Quarterly.$5.00/year.

*Civil Rights Organizations, Anti-war, Peace-action Groups/
Related Publications*

American Friends Service
   Committee
1501 Cherry Street
Philadelphia, Pennsylvania 19102

American Indian Movement
   (A.I.M.)
Information Office
Box 175
Porcupine, South Dakota 57772

Amnesty International, U.S.A.
12 Parker Street
Cambridge, Massachusetts 02138

Black Hills Alliance
Box 2508
Rapid City, South Dakota 57701

Campaign for Economic
   Democracy
304 South Broadway, Room 224
Los Angeles, California 90013

The Catholic Worker
36 East First Street
New York, New York 10003

Central Committee for
   Conscientious Objectors
2208 South Street
Philadelphia, Pennsylvania 19146

Children's Defense Fund
1520 New Hampshire Ave. N.W.
Washington, D.C. 20036

Citizens Against Nuclear Power
711 South Dearborn
Chicago, Illinois 60605

Citizens Against Nuclear Threats
106 Girard Street, S.E.
Albuquerque, New Mexico 87106

Clergy and Laity Concerned
198 Broadway
New York, New York 10038

Coalition for a New Foreign
   and Military Policy
120 Maryland Avenue, N.E.
Washington, D.C. 20002

Committee Against Registration
   and the Draft
245 Second Street, N.E.
Washington, D.C. 20002

The Fellowship of Reconciliation
Box 271
Nyack, New York 10960

Mobilization for Survival
East Coast:
3601 Locust Walk
Philadelphia, Pennsylvania 19104
West Coast:
944 Market Street, Room 808
San Francisco, California 94102

Movement for a New Society
4722 Baltimore Avenue
Philadelphia, Pennsylvania 19143

Musicians United for Safe
Energy (M.U.S.E.)
72 Fifth Avenue
New York, New York 10011

National Association for the
Advancement of Colored
People (NAACP)
National Office
1790 Broadway
New York, New York 10019

National Urban League
500 East Sixty-second Street
New York, New York 10021

Science for the People
897 Main Street
Cambridge, Massachusetts 02139

Union of Concerned Scientists
1384 Massachusetts Avenue
Cambridge, Massachusetts 02138

United Farmworkers of America
P.O. Box 62
Keene, California 93531

VISTA (Volunteers in Service to
America)
806 Connecticut Avenue
Washington, D.C. 20525

Vocations for Social Change
P.O. Box 211, Essex Station
Boston, Massachusetts 02112

War Resisters League
319 Lafayette Street
New York, New York 10012

Akwesasne Notes (Coverage of the struggles of Native American peoples), Mohawk Nation, via Rooseveltown, New York, 13683. No set subscription rate; send contribution. Monthly.

The Black Scholar (A monthly journal of black studies), Black World Foundation, P.O. Box 908, Sausalito, California, 94965. $12.00/year.

The Catholic Worker Newspaper (A publication of The Catholic Worker House), 36 East First Street, New York, New York, 10003. Monthly.25¢/year.

A Citizen's Guide on How to Use the Freedom of Information Act and the Privacy Act in Requesting Government Documents (Thirteenth Report by the Committee on Government Operations), 1977. Available from the Superintendent of Documents, U.S. Government Printing Office, Washington, D.C., 20402. $3.50.

Facing History and Ourselves: A Curriculum (Assists students and teachers in dealing with the Nazi Holocaust, and with their own moral decisions). Facing History, Brookline Public Schools, 25 Kennard Road, Brookline, MA 02146. 9 volumes/$15.00.

Feed, Need, Greed—Food Resources and Population: A High School Curriculum (Published by Science for the People, this curriculum encourages critical thinking and awareness in students and teachers regarding the corporate interests of the food distribution system and its relationship to hunger, population and resources.), $5.00.

"We Interrupt this Program": A Citizen's Guide to Using the Media for Social Change, by Robbie Gordon. Distributed by Volunteer Readership, P.O. Box 1807, Boulder, Colorado, 80306. $5.00.

Fellowship (A publication of the Fellowship of Reconciliation), Box 271, Nyack, New York, 10960. $6.00/year.

Freedomways (A quarterly review of the Freedom Movement), 799 Broadway, New York, New York, 10003. $4.50/year.

F.P.S.: A Magazine of Young People's Liberation, published and distributed by Youth Liberation, 2007 Washtenaw Avenue, Ann Arbor, Michigan, 48104. $10.00/6 issues.

In These Times (A weekly independent newspaper), published and distributed by the Institute for Policy Studies, 1509 North Milwaukee Avenue, Chicago, Illinois, 60622. $10.95/6 months; $19.50/year.

Peace Studies Institute Bulletin, % Peace Studies Institute, Manchester College, North Manchester, Indiana, 46962. Bi-annually. $3.00/year.

Science for the People (With special issues on "Science Teaching"), 897 Main Street, Cambridge, Massachusetts, 02139. Bi-monthly. $7.00/year.

Southern Exposure (Periodical of Southern struggles), published and distributed by the Institute for Southern Studies, P.O. Box 531, Durham, North Carolina, 27702. Quarterly.$10.00/year.

Win Magazine, Inc. (A weekly magazine dedicated to change through nonviolent action), 503 Atlantic Avenue, Fifth floor, Brooklyn, New York, 11217. $11.00/year.

Youth Alternatives (Advocates social change in youth services and focuses on issues that affect young people specifically), published and distributed by the National Youth Alternatives Project, 1346 Connecticut Avenue, N.W., Washington, D.C., 20036. Monthly. $10.00/individual; $20.00/institutions.

Third World Organizations/International Publications

American Committee on Africa
305 East Forty-sixth Street
New York, New York 10017

Indochina Resource Center
P.O. Box 4000 D
Berkeley, California 94704

Community Action on Latin
  America (CALA)
731 State Street
Madison, Wisconsin 53703

Nicaraguan Solidarity Committee
National Office
1322 Eighteenth Street
Washington, D.C. 20036

Center for Cuban Studies
220 East Twenty-third Street
New York, New York 10010

U.S. China People's Friendship
  Association
50 Oak Street, Room 502
San Francisco, California 94102

Cuba Resource Center
11 John Street, Room 506
New York, New York 10038

Washington Office on Latin
  America
110 Maryland Avenue, N.E.
Washington, D.C., 20002

Bulletin of Committee of Concerned Asian Scholars, P.O. Box W, Charlemont, Massachusetts 01139. $8.00/year; $6.00/students.

Chile Newsletter: NICH—Non Intervention in Chile (A bi-monthly publication with updated information on Chile), Box 800, Berkeley, California, 94701. $5.00/individual; $10.00/institution.

China Books and Periodicals (National agency for publications in English from the People's Republic of China), 125 Fifth Avenue, New York, New York, 10003; 2929 Twenty-fourth Street, San Francisco, California, 94110. Send for free catalogue.

Cuba Times (A publication of the Cuba Resource Center), 11 John Street, Room 506, New York, New York, 10038

Cuba Update (A publication of the Center for Cuban Studies), 220 East Twenty-third Street, New York, New York, 10010

Dollars and Sense (Reviews the national and international economic situation from a socialist perspective), 324 Somerville Avenue, Somerville, Massachusetts, 02143. Monthly. $5.00/yr.

Latin American Perspectives, % CSMI, P.O. Box 792, Riverside, California, 92502. $10.00/year.

Middle East Research and Information Project Bulletin (MERIP) (A journal which focuses on the role of the United States in the political economies of Middle Eastern countries), P.O. Box 48, Harvard Square Station, Cambridge, Massachusetts, 02138. Monthly. $6.00/year.

North American Congress on Latin America (NACLA Report), Box 57, Cathedral Park Station, New York, New York, 10025. Write for free literature.

People Acting for Change Together (PACT) (Provides resource material on Third World issues, women's issues and racism), 163 Madison, Detroit, Michigan, 48226. $10.00/10 packets.

UNESCO Publications, % The United Nations, New York, New York, 10017.

Bibliography

This is a selected bibliography. Many of the books listed here have been referred to in the text. Other books are listed because of their relevance to the issues raised in the text and therefore should be of special interest to teachers, students and parents.

General Interest

Adoff, Arnold ed. *Black on Black: Commentaries by Black Americans from Frederick Douglas to Malcolm X*. New York: The Macmillan Company, 1968.

Board of Education, City of New York. *Regulations Governing the Collection, Maintenance and Dissemination of Student Records*. 1973.

Bowles, Samuel and Gintis, Herbert. *Schooling in Capitalist America*. New York: Basic Books, Inc., 1976.

Braun, Robert. *Teachers and Power*. New York: Simon and Schuster, 1972.

Carnoy, Martin. *Education as Cultural Imperialism*. New York: McKay Publishers, 1974.

Channon, Gloria. *Homework*. New York: Outerbridge and Dienstfrey, 1970.

Clark, Kenneth. *Dark Ghetto*. New York: Harper and Row, 1965.

Coles, Robert and Berrigan, Daniel. *The Geography of Faith*. Boston: Beacon Press, 1970.

Cremin, Lawrence. *The Transformation of the School*. New York: Vintage Books, 1964.

Counts, George. *Dare the School Build a New Social Order?* New York: John Day Company, 1968.

Dewey, John. *Democracy and Education*. New York: The Free Press, 1968.

Fantini, Mario. *Public Schools of Choice.* New York: Simon and Schuster, Inc., 1974.

Freire, Paulo. *Pedagogy of the Oppressed.* New York: Seabury Press, 1970.

Freire, Paulo. *Education for Critical Consciousness.* New York: Continuum Books, 1980.

Freire, Paulo. *Pedagogy in Process.* New York: Seabury Press, 1978.

Friedenberg, Edgar. *The Dignity of Youth.* Boston: Beacon Press, 1966.

Gerassi, John. *The Great Fear in Latin America.* New York: Macmillan Company, 1963.

Glasser, William, M.D. *Schools Without Failure.* New York: Harper and Row, Publishers, 1969.

Goodman, Paul. *Compulsory Mis-Education.* New York: Vintage Books, 1966.

Goodman, Paul. *Growing Up Absurd.* New York: Vintage Books, 1970.

Greer, Colin. *The Great School Legend.* New York: Basic Books, Inc., 1970.

Greer, Colin, ed. *The Solution as Part of the Problem.* New York: Harper and Row, 1973.

Gross, Ronald and Osterman, Paul, eds. *High School.* New York: Simon and Schuster, 1971.

Holt, John. *The Under-Achieving School.* New York: Dell Publishing Company, 1969.

Henry, Jules. *Culture Against Man.* New York: Vintage Books, 1965.

Jencks, Christopher. *Inequality.* New York: Basic Books, Inc., 1972.

Katz, Michael. *The Irony of Early School Reform.* Boston: Beacon Press, 1968.

Katz, Michael. *Class, Bureaucracy and Schools.* New York: Praeger Publishing Company, 1975.

Keniston, Kenneth. *The Uncommitted.* New York: Harcourt, Brace and World, Inc., 1965.

Keniston, Kenneth. *Young Radicals.* New York: Harcourt, Brace and World, Inc., 1968.

Kozol, Jonathan. *Death at an Early Age.* New York: Bantam Books, 1968.

Kozol, Jonathan. *The Night Is Dark and I Am Far From Home.* New York: Continuum Books, 1980.

Lessing, Doris. *The Golden Notebook.* New York: Bantam Books, 1973.

Levine, Alan H., with Carey, Eve and Divocky, Diane. *The Rights of Students*. New York: Avon Books, 1973.

Lurie, Ellen. How to Change the Schools: *A Parent's Action Handbook on How to Fight the System*. New York: Vintage Books, 1970.

Marciano, John and Griffin, William L. *Teaching the Vietnam War*. New Jersey: Allanheld, Osmun & Company, 1980.

Merrill, Walter and Ruchames, Louis. *The Letters of William Lloyd Garrison*. 5 volumes. Massachusetts: Harvard University Press, 1971–1979.

Nelson, Truman. *The Old Man*. New York: Holt, Rinehart and Winston, 1973.

Nelson, Truman. *The Right of Revolution*. Boston: Beacon Press, 1968.

Nelson, Truman. *The Sin of the Prophet*. Boston: Little, Brown and Company, 1952.

Petras, James. *Politics and Social Structure in Latin America*. New York: Monthly Review Press, 1970.

Ravitch, Diane. *The Great School Wars*. New York: Harper and Row, 1974.

Rubin, David. *The Rights of Teachers*. New York: Avon Books, 1971.

Scribner, Harvey B. and Stevens, Leonard B. *Make Your Schools Work*. New York: Simon and Schuster Publishing Company, 1975.

Shor, Ira. *Critical Teaching and Everyday Life*. Boston: South End Press, 1980.

Spring, Joel. *Education and the Rise of the Corporate State*. Boston: Beacon Press, 1972.

Spring, Joel. *A Primer on Libertarian Education*. New York: Free Life Publishers, 1975.

Thoreau, Henry David. *Walden* and *On the Duty of Civil Disobedience*. New York: Holt, Rinehart and Winston, Inc., 1948.

Wasserman, Miriam. *Demystifying School*. New York: Praeger Publishers, 1973.

Wasserman, Miriam and Hutchinson, Linda. *Teaching Human Dignity*. Minneapolis: The Education Exploration Center, 1978.

Wynia, Gary W. *The Politics of Latin American Development*. New York: Cambridge University Press, 1978.

Women in History

Ahlum, Carol and Fralley, Jacqueline. *High School Feminist Studies: A Curriculum*. New York: The Feminist Press, 1977.

Ashbaugh, Carol. *Lucy Parsons: American Revolutionary*. Chicago: Charles H. Kerr Publishing Company, 1976.

Bradford, Sarah. *Harriet Tubman: The Moses of her People*. New Jersey: The Citadel Press, 1974.

Buckmaster, Henrietta. *Women Who Shaped History*. New York: Collier Books, 1966.

Day, Dorothy. *The Long Loneliness: The Autobiography of Dorothy Day*. New York: Harper and Brothers, 1952.

Day, Dorothy. *House of Hospitality*. New York: Sheed and Ward, Inc., 1939.

Day, Dorothy. *Loaves and Fishes*. New York: Harper and Row, 1963.

Foner, Phillip S. *Helen Keller: Her Socialist Years*. New York: International Publishers, 1967.

Gates, Barbara; Klaw, Susan; and Steinberg, Adria. *Changing Learning/Changing Lives: A High School Women's Studies Curriculum from The Group School*. New York: The Feminist Press, 1979.

Harrison, Barbara Grizzuti. *Unlearning the Lie: Sexism in School*. New York: Morrow Paperback Editions, 1973.

Jacobs, Sue-Ellen. *Women in Perspective: A Guide for Cross-Cultural Studies*. Chicago: University of Illinois Press, 1976.

Jones, Mary H. *The Autobiography of Mother Jones*. Chicago: Charles H. Kerr Publishing Company, 1972.

Lerner, Gerda. *The Woman in American History*. Massachusetts: Addison-Wesley, Publishers, 1971.

Lerner, Gerda. *Black Women in White America: A Documentary History*. New York: Vintage Books, 1972.

Miller, William D. *A Harsh and Dreadful Love: Dorothy Day and The Catholic Worker Movement*. New York: Liveright Publishing Company, 1973.

Rowbotham, Sheila. *Woman's Consciousness, Man's World*. New York: Penguin Books, 1973.

Rowbotham, Sheila. *Women: Resistance and Revolution*. London: Allen Lane Publishers, 1972.

Schniedewind, Nancy. *Confronting Racism and Sexism: A Practical Handbook for Educators*. New York: Common Ground Press, 1977.

Stacey, Judith; Bereaud, Susan; and Daniels, Joan, eds. *And Jill Came Tumbling After: Sexism in American Education*. New York: Dell Publishing Company, 1974.

History From the Bottom Up

Boyer, Richard O., and Morais, Herbert. *Labor's Untold Story*. Published by the United Electrical Workers, 1971.

Douglas, Frederick. *My Bondage and My Freedom*. New York: Arno Press, 1968.

Fanon, Frantz. *The Wretched of the Earth*. New York: Grove Press, 1965.

Gendzier, Irene L. *Frantz Fanon: A Critical Study*. New York: Vintage Books, 1974.

Gregory, Dick. *No More Lies: The Myth and Reality of American History*. New York: Harper and Row, 1971.

King, Martin Luther. *Stride Toward Freedom*. New York: Harper and Row, 1958.

Lynd, Alice and Lynd, Staughton, eds. *Rank and File: Personal Histories by Working-Class Organizers*. Boston: Beacon Press, 1973.

Lynd, Staughton, ed. *Nonviolence in America: A Documentary History*. Indianapolis: The Bobbs Merrill Company, Inc., 1966.

Meltzer, Milton. *Bread and Roses: The Struggle of American Labor, 1865–1915*. New York: Vintage Books, 1973.

Neuhaus, Richard J. and Berger, Peter L. *Movement and Revolution*. New York: Doubleday and Company, Inc., 1970.

Padover, Saul K., ed. *Thomas Jefferson's "Democracy."* New York: Greenwood Press, 1969.

Quarles, Benjamin, ed. *Frederick Douglas*. New Jersey: Prentice-Hall, Inc., 1968.

Terkel, Studs. *Working*. New York: Avon Books, 1975.

Terkel, Studs. *Hard Times*. New York: Pocket Books, 1978.

Malcolm X. *The Autobiography of Malcolm X*. New York: Ballantine Books, 1964.

Wasserman, Harvey. *Harvey Wasserman's History of the United States*. New York: Harper and Row, 1972.

Zinn, Howard. *Disobedience and Democracy*. New York: Vintage Books, 1968.

Zinn, Howard. *A People's History of the United States*. New York: Harper and Row, 1980.

Zinn, Howard. *The Politics of History*. Boston: Beacon Press, 1970.

Books on Teaching Reading

Ashton-Warner, Sylvia. *Teacher*. New York: Bantam Books, 1964.

Baratz, Joan C. and Shuy, Roger W. *Teaching Black Children to*

Read. Published by the Center for Applied Linguistics, Washington, D.C., 1969.

Chall, Jeanne. *Learning to Read: The Great Debate*. New York: McGraw-Hill Book Company, 1967.

Dennison, George. *The Lives of Children*. New York: Vintage Books, 1970.

Fader, Daniel. *Hooked On Books*. New York: Berkeley Publishing Corporation, 1976.

Gray, Lillian. *Teaching Children to Read*. New York: Roland Press, 1963.

Herndon, James. *How to Survive in Your Native Land*. New York: Simon and Schuster, 1971.

Koch, Kenneth. *Wishes, Lies and Dreams*. New York: Vintage Books, 1970.

Kohl, Herbert. *Reading: How To*. New York: Bantam Books, 1974.

Means, Harrison. "Nine Years of Individualized Reading," *Journal of Reading,* November, 1976.

Moffett, James and Wagner, Betty J. *Student-Centered Language Arts and Reading, K-13: A Handbook for Teachers*. Boston: Houghton-Mifflin Company, 1976.

Smith, Frank. *Reading Without Nonsense*. New York: Teachers College Press, 1978.

Spaulding, Romalda. *The Writing Road to Reading*. New York: William Morrow Publishing Company, 1969.

Williams, Frederick, ed. *Language and Poverty*. New York: Academic Press, Inc., 1970.

Notes

1. Doris Lessing is quoted from *The Golden Notebook*. See the author's special introduction in the Bantam edition (New York: Bantam Books, 1973), p. xvii.
2. Quotations from the Arizona Board of Education are extracted from the "Preamble to U.S. Course of Study," adopted by the Arizona Board on September 21, 1972. This document is no longer available to the public. According to Dr. Thomas Reno, Associate Superintendent, the document was replaced in 1976 by a revised and sanitized version. Unhappily, it is the original version which most faithfully reflects the characteristic goals and guidelines of the U.S. public schools.
3. Massachusetts educator Horace Mann is quoted from *The Republic and the School: Horace Mann on the Education Of Free Men,* edited by Lawrence A. Cremin (New York: Teachers College Press, Columbia University, 1957). A more accessible source for the same quotation is *The Great School Legend* by Colin Greer (New York: Basic Books, Inc., 1972), p. 75.
4. Sentimentalists and purblind patriots, who do not like to think ill of their former presidents, will be quick to pounce upon a shocking quotation of this kind and to insist that it is "taken out of context"and so cannot conceivably reflect "the true opinions" of its author. All the more reason, then, why teachers and writers must be extremely careful in their selection of such statements, in order to be sure that they, in fact, *do* represent the true convictions of their speakers/authors. In the case of Wilson, a small amount of research will unearth an ever-increasing volume of disturbing insight into his aristocratic and class-serving point of view. "Undoubtedly," said Wilson, in a speech delivered in Cambridge, Massachusetts in 1909, "the education which gives them [i.e., the masses of the nation] skill of hand and acquaintance

with all the means by which advancement in the practical arts are to be attained . . . is an indispensable necessity. Schools of technical training are not only desirable but indispensable, and the greater part of the education which a nation attempts must be of that kind, because that is the sort of education most universally needed—needed, I mean, by the largest number of persons. But we are not to stop there, and we are not to put our minds in confusion by placing that sort of education in competition or contrast with that which has for its object, not technical skill, but sheer enlargement of the mind. . . . And so we feel that we are entitled to be full of hope in regard to the increasing intellectual life of Princeton. I am covetous for Princeton of all the glory that there is, and the chief glory of a university is always intellectual glory. The chief glory of a university is the leadership of the nation in the things that attach to the highest ambitions that nations can set themselves, those ideals which lift nations into the atmosphere of things that are permanent and do not fade from generation to generation. I do not see how any man can fail to perceive that scholarship, that education in a country like ours, is a branch of statemanship. It is a branch of that general work of enabling a great country to use its energies to the best advantage and to lift itself from generation to generation through stages of unbroken progress. . . . No man can do anything in his generation by and of himself. He must rule his fellow-men and draw them into cooperation with himself, if he would accomplish anything. There is a touch of modern statesmanship about every piece of modern business. . . . It is as if all the powers of the world were organized and the captains of industry were making their way forward in the ranks to be generals in command of the forces of mankind. . . ." See *The Politics of Woodrow Wilson*, edited by August Heckscher (New York: Harper and Row, 1956), pp. 138, 142, 143.

5. Thomas Jefferson orginally wrote these words in a letter, dated 1787. The quotation can be found in *Democracy*, edited by Saul K. Padover (New York: Greenwood Press, 1969), p. 259.

6. William Lloyd Garrison's words are quoted from *The Politics of History* by Howard Zinn (Boston: Beacon Press, 1970), p. 147.

7. Henry David Thoreau is quoted from *Walden*. See *Walden* and *On the Duty of Civil Disobedience* (New York: Holt, Rinehart and Winston, Inc., 1948), pp. 270–71.

8. Martin Luther King, Jr.'s "Letter from Birmingham Jail" is re-

printed in *Nonviolence in America*, edited by Staughton Lynd (Indianapolis: The Bobbs Merrill Company, Inc., 1966), p. 474.

9. The quotation on obedience is taken from "Curriculum Guide in Character Education," School Document Number 11, 1962. See *Death at an Early Age* (Bantam Books: New York, 1968), p. 180.

10. The National Education Association guidebook is entitled *Discipline in the Classroom* (National Education Association, 1969), p. 39. See also *Controlling Classroom Misbehavior* (National Education Association, 1973).

11. The passage on Helen Keller quoted here is a pastiche of standard biographical works on Keller used in public schools.

12. Helen Keller is quoted from an essay written in 1913 entitled "New Vision for the Blind." See *Helen Keller: Her Socialist Years* by Philip S. Foner (New York: International Publishers, 1967), pp. 55–56.

13. The quotation on elections by Helen Keller can be found in *Helen Keller: Her Socialist Years*, p. 31.

14. Martin Luther King, Jr., is quoted here from *Movement and Revolution*, by Richard J. Neuhaus and Peter L. Berger (New York: Doubleday and Company, Inc., 1970), p. 97.

15. J. Edgar Hoover's blackmail of Dr. King is documented in *The Boston Globe*, September 3, 1975.

16. Martin Luther King, Jr. is paraphrased from *The Little Red, White and Blue Book*, edited by J. A. Rossen, (New York: Grove Press, 1969), p. 42.

17. Henry David Thoreau is quoted throughout this chapter from *Civil Disobedience*. See *Walden* and *On the Duty of Civil Disobedience*, pp. 284–85.

18. Abraham Lincoln is quoted from a speech delivered in southern Illinois in 1858. For this and other annotated material on Lincoln, see *The Politics of History*, p. 148.

19. According to the *Digest of Educational Statistics*, there were 42,900,000 students enrolled in our public education system in the 1977 academic year. This figure includes elementary and secondary students. Students in private, parochial and special schools are not incorporated in the total.

20. Since 1974, with the passage of the Family Education Rights and Privacy Act (otherwise known as The Buckley Amendment, named after its chief sponsor Senator James Buckley of New York), parents and students have had legal right of access to inspect and review "education records," defined as "those records,

files, documents and other materials which (a) contain information directly related to a student and (b) are maintained by an educational agency or by a person acting for such an agency or institution." Records are broadly defined to include "any information or data recorded in any medium, including but not limited to handwriting, print, tapes, microfilm and microfiche." There are some exceptions as to what can be examined by student or parent; but these exceptions are so few that they do not represent a substantial limitation on the right of access to all records of concern. As mentioned in the text, schools will sometimes keep a second set of records of which few parents are aware, but the 1974 legislation now insists that schools inform parents of "all types" of records maintained. For quoted material and additional information on The Buckley Amendment (including specifics regarding its limitations) see *Inequality in Education,* Volume 22, July 1977, published by The Center for Law and Education, Harvard University, 6 Appian Way, Cambridge, Massachusetts, 02138.

21. The court case affirming the right of refusal to recite the Pledge of Allegiance in school took place in West Virginia in 1943. In this landmark case, *West Virginia* vs. *Barnette,* it was determined that "the action of a State in making it compulsory for children in the public schools to salute the flag and pledge allegiance . . . violates the First and Fourteenth Amendments" (see citing 319 U.S. 624 at p. 642). For more recent cases, see *Hamilton* vs. *The Board of Regents* (293 U.S. 245), *Banks* vs. *Board of Public Instruction of Dade County, Florida* (314, Federal Supplement, 285) in 1970, *Goetz* vs. *Ansell* (477, F 2nd, 636) in 1973. For an account of one student who refused the flag pledge and won vindication in the courts, see "Girl's Flag Carrying Called 'Illegal,' 'Bizarre,' " *Boston Globe,* November 18, 1970. Another case, involving the refusal of a teacher to recite the pledge, is documented in an excellent article, "A Teacher's Right to Shun the Flag Pledge," *New York Times,* February 18, 1974.

22. For further information on certain of our oldest U.S. allies in the Latin nations, see *The Great Fear in Latin America,* by John Gerassi (New York: Macmillan Company, 1963). For more recent information see *Politics and Social Structure in Latin America,* by James Petras (New York: Monthly Review Press, 1970) and *The Politics of Latin American Development,* by Gary C. Wynia (New York: Cambridge University Press, 1978).

23. *The American Statistical Index for 1980,* published by the Congressional Information Service in Washington, D.C., refers the reader to the *Foreign Military Sales and Military Assistance Figures* for 1979, which lists the 93 nations with which the United States has military sales agreements.

24. John Milton is quoted from *The Areopagitica*. See *The Complete Prose of John Milton,* Volume 2, edited by Ernest Sirluck (Connecticut: Yale University Press, 1959), p. 561.

25. Statistics and documentation on South Africa are drawn from an article which ran in *The Boston Globe* on January 25, 1970. See "South Africa's arsenal grows, despite U.N. embargo plea," by Darius Jhalaba.

26. For a recent description of teacher centers funded and organized by the two major educational associations (the N.E.A. and the A.F.T.) see "Teacher Centers: Best Effort Yet at Upgrading Teachers," *Boston Globe*, August 3, 1980.

27. Senator George McGovern is quoted from a speech delivered on International Literacy Day, September 8, 1978. See *The Congressional Record,* Proceedings and Debates of the Ninety-fifth Congress, Second Session, Volume 124, Number 139, Washington, D.C.

28. *Lies,* by Yevgeny Yevtushenko, is included in *Yevtushenko: Selected Poems,* translated by Robin Milner-Gulland (New York: E. P. Dutton and Company, Inc., 1962), p. 52.